Cataloging Correctly for Kids

An Introduction to the Tools

THIRD EDITION

Sharon Zuiderveld

Editor

AMERICAN LIBRARY ASSOCIATION
Chicago and London 1998

Design and composition by Dianne M. Rooney in Garamond Book and Friz Quadrata using QuarkXPress 3.32 on a Power Macintosh 8500/180

Printed on 50-pound White Offset, a pH-neutral stock, and bound in 10-point coated cover stock by Victor Graphics

The paper used in this publication meets the minimum requirements of American National Standard for Information Sciences—Permanence of Paper for Printed Library Materials, ANSI Z39.48-1992.

Library of Congress Cataloging-in-Publication Data

Cataloging correctly for kids : an introduction to the tools / Sharon
    Zuiderveld, editor. — 3rd ed.
       p.   cm.
    Includes bibliographical references (p.).
    ISBN 0-8389-3476-5
    1. Cataloging of children's literature—United States.
  I. Zuiderveld, Sharon.
  Z695.1.C6C37   1998
  025.3'2—dc21   97-41145

Printed in the United States of America.

02   01   ·   5   4   3

Contents

Preface

THE SUCCESS OF THE FIRST two editions of *Cataloging Correctly for Kids* encouraged me to spur on the members of the Cataloging of Children's Materials Committee to revise, revamp, or write completely new articles for this edition. Knowing that school library media specialists and children's librarians found the book useful led us to approach the Association of Library Resources and Technical Services Division to place the publication in print again.

Many thanks are due the authors for their diligence; Diane Stine, chair of the Cataloging of Children's Materials Committee, for her assistance; Ann Case for her capable editorial scrutiny of the Guidelines; Gregory New for his unfailing attention to detail in perusing the manuscript with me; Margaret Rohdy, chair of the ALCTS Publications Committee, for steering the manuscript through the shoals of peer readership; Robert F. Sibert and Robert L. Sibert of Bound to Stay Bound Books for their encouragement and support; and, finally, Jim Braden, programmer extraordinaire at Bound to Stay Bound Books, for merging many discs and word-processing programs into a coherent whole.

Introduction

Gregory R. New

THE CATALOGING OF CHILDREN'S Materials Committee takes pride in presenting a third edition of *Cataloging Correctly for Kids.* This edition, like the first edition published in 1989, is designed for two fundamental purposes. First, it provides a readily available home for the most recent revision of "Guidelines for Standardized Cataloging of Children's Materials," which has been the ALA standard since 1982. But even more important, it provides librarians with much needed help in achieving quality cataloging of material for which LC-based cataloging is not available.

Cataloging Correctly for Kids consists of the Guidelines and a set of brief articles that help catalogers use standard tools and take advantage of recognized sources for standardized in-house cataloging. Libraries can now achieve high standards in a cost-effective manner. The authors (other than myself) are current or former catalogers of children's materials. Building upon their experience, they emphasize tools that enable librarians to provide quick access to children's col lections and to create permanent records comparable with other records within the larger information system in which children and their librarians work.

The Guidelines are the basic element upon which all the articles are built. They were originally prepared by the Cataloging of Children's Materials Committee and adopted by ALA in 1982, and were revised in 1986, 1990, and 1996. They essentially spell out the particulars of the principle adopted by the Committee in 1969, that Library of Congress cataloging practices for children's materials be adopted as a national standard. While the Committee reaffirms the importance of standards embodied in LC practice, several individual articles discuss alternatives that have been widely accepted, such as *Sears List of Subject Headings,* or offer personal evaluations.

Much has happened in the library world since the second edition appeared in 1991, and we needed to revise the Guidelines and several of the articles again. We are also adding new articles that reflect an increasing range of problems with which children's librarians now cope: Authority Control, How Children Search, Sources for Dewey Numbers, and Curriculum-Enhanced MARC.

For the most part, each of the articles can stand alone and be read separately. Each author writes from his or her own perspective that does not necessarily reflect the views of the Committee. However, the articles are interconnected, and each answers questions related to the others. They flow in a natural sequence from the general or familiar to the specific or specialized:

1. *The Guidelines:* The outline elaborates the Library of Congress practices that have become the standard.

2. *The Annotated Card Program:* Jane Gilchrist of the LC Children's Literature Team gives the background of LC practice and offers examples.

3. *Vendors of Cataloging for Children's Materials:* Betty Vandivier and two past Committee members list some of the prime sources from which many children's libraries get standard cataloging.

4. *How the CIP Program Helps Children's Librarians:* Susan Vita explains a direct source children's librarians use.

5. *Using AACR2R in Cataloging Children's Collections:* Sharon Zuiderveld offers basic information on descriptive cataloging rules.

6. *Authority Control:* Ruth Bogan tells how catalogers standardize the terms and cross-references by which people look up information in catalogs.

7. *How Children Search:* Lynne Jacobsen offers forward-looking suggestions for developing new systems to help children look up information.

8. *Dewey Considerations:* Frances Corcoran describes the basic subject classification tool and tells how it may be adapted to serve local needs.

9. *Sources for Dewey Numbers:* Gregory New tells where to find reliable DDC numbers.

10. *Sears List of Subject Headings:* Joseph Miller describes a widely used alternative source of subject headings.

11. *Cataloging Nonbook Materials:* Jean Weihs discusses cataloging the wide variety of formats so that all material can be represented in one catalog.

Finally, a bibliography lists the primary tools, more articles on cataloging for children, and suggestions for further reading and study.

1

Guidelines for Standardized Cataloging of Children's Materials

Association for Library Collections and Technical Services/CCS Cataloging of Children's Materials Committee

THE LIBRARY COMMUNITY has long recognized that the users of children's materials have their own unique characteristics and requirements. Children's materials, both print and nonprint, are considered different enough from general materials to warrant special bibliographic treatment to meet the needs of the audience for which they are intended.

Background

In recognition of the unique nature of juvenile materials and in response to the needs of the users of these materials, the Library of Congress established the Annotated Card (AC) Program in 1966. Currently administered by the Children's Literature Team of the Library of Congress History and Literature Cataloging Division, the program has adapted the Library's cataloging policies and practices to include annotations, modified subject headings, and some special classification numbers. The Annotated Card Program was made accessible through catalog cards from the Library of Congress and

The Guidelines were approved by the ALCTS Board of Directors, June 28, 1997.

later through MARC (Machine-Readable Cataloging) records and the Cataloging in Publication program.

During the 1960s, as libraries found it cheaper or more convenient to rely on commercial or centralized processing services, it became apparent that standardization of cataloging practices was necessary. A study by the Cataloging of Children's Materials Committee of the Resources and Technical Services Division of the American Library Association found that the lack of a uniform standard meant that many libraries developed custom cataloging according to their own perceived needs or accepted nonstandard cataloging from other sources.

The cost of customized cataloging, however, cut into other services, and if the source of cataloging changed, so did the style and standard of cataloging. The Committee also foresaw that the development of the MARC program and nationwide bibliographic utilities offered potential for the wider dissemination of standardized cataloging, provided that guidelines for standardization could be developed and followed. In response, the Cataloging of Children's Materials Committee recommended in 1969 that the Library of Congress cataloging practices for children's materials be adopted as a national standard. This recommendation was subsequently adopted by the Cataloging and Classification Section of the Resources and Technical Services Division, renamed Association for Library Collections and Technical Services (ALCTS) in 1989.

As more libraries began to benefit from shared cataloging efforts, either directly through bibliographic utilities or indirectly through commercial processors who used MARC records, it became advantageous in terms of cost and data compatibility to accept this standardization. The creation and exchange of bibliographic data at an international level, and access to these data by commercial processors as well as by libraries, made a deficiency apparent: although the American Library Association accepted the Library of Congress's cataloging of children's materials as a standard, there had never been a codification of this standard accessible to all who wished to follow it. In 1982, the Cataloging of Children's Materials Committee, with the cooperation of the Children's Literature Section (since renamed the Children's Literature Team) of the Library of Congress, developed the Guidelines herein for standardized cataloging of children's materials, which were accepted by the RTSD Board of Directors on July 14, 1982.

Since 1982, MARC records have become even more readily available and widely used because of the growing automation of smaller libraries. Libraries of all sizes are converting from card catalogs to online public access catalogs. They are purchasing MARC records for retrospective conversion of their collections and acquiring current records from their materials vendors or from vendors of cataloging data for use with commercially available microcomputer programs. Given the continued need for standards understood by the cataloger, the materials vendor, the cataloging data vendor, and the software producer—and in view of changes in cataloging policy and practice—the Cataloging of Children's Materials Committee revised and updated these Guidelines in 1996.

Scope

The Guidelines are intended for use in cataloging all materials deemed intellectually suitable for children. The matter of deciding what materials are suitable for inclusion in a juvenile collection may be difficult and subjective. For purposes of these Guidelines, consider as juvenile those works intended by the author or publisher, or deemed suitable by the cataloger, for use by children and young people through ninth grade (age 15). Application of these Guidelines to materials for grades 10 through 12 is optional.

Agencies that contribute cataloging to a shared database using the MARC format must place an appropriate code in the fixed-field character position for target audience (008/22). The code j indicates that the item is intended for use by children and young people through the age of 15 or the ninth grade. The code a, b, c, or d may be used when a more specific description of the juvenile audience is desired. If an item is appropriate for more than one audience, the code for the principal target audience is assigned. Following is an explanation of the codes:

a   Preschool (up to, but not including, kindergarten)
b   Primary (kindergarten through third grade)
c   Elementary and junior high (grades 4 through 8)
d   Secondary [senior high] (grades 9 through 12)
j   Juvenile (through age 15 or grade 9)

These Guidelines are compatible with national cataloging tools and should be used in conjunction with them. Currently, these tools include *Anglo-American Cataloguing Rules,* second edition, 1988 revision, with 1993 amendments (AACR2R), and interpretations of them by the Library of Congress (as published in *Library of Congress Rule Interpretations* (LCRI)); *Library of Congress Subject Headings* (LCSH), current edition, including Annotated Card Program modifications, and principles for applying them (as published in *Subject Cataloging Manual: Subject Headings*); Dewey Decimal Classification schedules (abridged); and Library of Congress Classification schedules. These Guidelines present the practices of the Library of Congress for cataloging children's material and note or expand on certain rules and options in AACR2R. Rules, options, and practices not touched upon are not meant to be excluded. References within this text to individual rules are to rules in AACR2R. Although instructions for MARC coding are not included in AACR2R, relevant MARC field numbers and subfield codes are identified in the Guidelines. Further information about MARC encoding may be found in the *USMARC Format for Bibliographic Data* or in local system manuals. The most commonly used USMARC fields are listed in Figure 1.

Figure 1.   Commonly Used USMARC Bibliographic Fields

010	Library of Congress Control Number (LCCN)
020	International Standard Book Number (ISBN)
050	Library of Congress Call Number
082	Dewey Decimal Call Number
100	Main entry—personal name
110	Main entry—corporate name
130	Main entry—uniform title
245	Title statement
246	Varying form of title
250	Edition statement
260	Publication, distribution, etc.
300	Physical description

440	Series statement/added entry—title
490	Series statement/not traced or traced differently
500	General note
501	With note
505	Formatted contents note
508	Creation/Production credits note
511	Participant or performer note
518	Date/Time and Place of an event note
520	Summary, etc. note
521	Target audience note
538	System details note
586	Awards note
600	Subject added entry—personal name
650	Subject added entry—topical term
651	Subject added entry—geographic name
658	Index term—Curriculum Objective
700	Added entry—personal name
710	Added entry—corporate name
730	Added entry—uniform title
830	Series added entry—uniform title

Guidelines for Description and Access

These Guidelines address the following:

> Description
> Name, title, and series access points
> Subject headings
> Classification

Examples of annotated catalog cards in AACR2R form with corresponding MARC records are given in Figures 2-5.

Figure 2.   Example of Annotated Catalog Card for a Book

Cushman, Karen.
    The midwife's apprentice / by Karen Cushman. — New York :
Clarion Books, c1995.
        122 p. ; 19 cm.
        Summary: In medieval England, a nameless, homeless girl is taken in
by a sharp-tempered midwife, and in spite of obstacles and hardship,
eventually gains the three things she most wants: a full belly, a con-
tented heart, and a place in this world.
        ISBN 0-395-69229-6
        Dewey Class No.: [Fic]—dc 20
        1. Middle Ages—Fiction.   2. Midwives—Fiction.   I. Title.
AACR 2
LC 940407 DLC   94–13792 /AC
DLT: 1996040   DLC   MARC

Figure 3.   USMARC Record for a Book

Leader	*****pam_22*****_a_4500
001	94013792 /AC
003	DLC
005	19960403112919.9
008	940407s1995_____nyu_____j_____000_1_eng__
010 __	$a 94013792 /AC
020 __	$a 0395692296
040 __	$a DLC $c DLC $d DLC
050 00	$a PZ7 .C962 $b Mi 1995
082 00	$a [Fic] $2 20
100 1_	$a Cushman, Karen.
245 14	$a The midwife's apprentice / $c by Karen Cushman.
260 __	$a New York : $b Clarion Books, $c c1995.
300 __	$a 122 p. ; $c 19 cm.
520 __	$a In medieval England, a nameless, homeless girl is taken in by a sharp-tempered midwife, and in spite of obstacles and hardship, eventually gains the three things she most wants: a full belly, a contented heart, and a place in this world.
650 _1	$a Middle Ages $x Fiction.
650 _1	$a Midwives $x Fiction.

Figure 4. Example of Annotated Catalog Card for a Nonbook Item

AE5

Microsoft Encarta [interactive multimedia] : multimedia
    encyclopedia. — [Redmond, Wash.] : Microsoft, c1993.
      1 computer optical disc : sd., col. ; 4 3/4 in. + 1 getting
    started manual (vii, 38 p.) + 1 research ideas/copyright
    responsibilities guide (v, 41 p.).
      (Windows series)
      Title from disc label.
      Summary: Presents the complete Funk & Wagnalls new
encyclopedia plus assorted sounds, music, spoken text, animation,
illustrations, photographs, maps, and additional printed material.
Features include topic tracker, hypertext category browser, bookmark
and note functions, and interactive atlas and timeline. Most textual and
visual material can be enlarged, copied, and printed for creating
reports.
      Dewey Class No.: 031—dc 12
      1. Electronic encyclopedias.   I. Microsoft Corporation.
II. Funk & Wagnalls new encyclopedia.

LC 950313 DLC   95-790234 / /r963
DLT: 1996041 DLC   MARC

Description

The description of the material to be cataloged must follow the second or third level of description as found in Rule 1.0D2 in AACR2R. Although many libraries have previously used abbreviated cataloging similar to the first level of description, the first level of description does not provide for elements that are considered important by many libraries and therefore are required by these Guidelines. These elements include statements of responsibility (including subsequent statements of responsibility such as "illustrated by . . . "), dimensions, and series. Elements that require clarification or for which specific treatment is suggested are discussed more fully below.

GMD

The General Material Designation (GMD) (Rule 1.1C) (subfield h of MARC field 245) is optional in AACR2R and selectively supplied in LCRI, but is strongly recommended in these Guidelines for all types

Figure 5.   USMARC Record for a Nonbook Item

Leader		*****cmm_22*****__4500
001		95790234 / /r963
003		DLC
005		19960410090740.8
008		950313s1993____waua____m_____eng__
010	__	$a 95790234 / /r963
040	__	$a DLC $c DLC $d DLC
050	00	$a AE5
082	10	$a 031 $2 12
245	00	$a Microsoft Encarta $h [interactive multimedia] : $b multimedia encyclopedia.
246	30	$a Encarta
256	__	$a Computer data and program.
260	__	$a [Redmond, Wash.] : $b Microsoft, $c c1993.
300	__	$a 1 computer optical disc : $b sd., col. ; $c 4 3/4 in. + $e 1 getting started manual (vii, 38 p.) + 1 research ideas/copyright responsibilities guide (v, 41 p.).
440	_0	$a Windows series
538	__	$a System requirements: Multimedia PC (or PC with Multimedia PC upgrade kit) with 386SX microprocessor or higher; 2 MB RAM; MS-DOS 3.1 or later; Microsoft Windows 3.1 or later; VGA graphics capabilities or better; 30MB hard disk; CD-ROM drive; audio board; Microsoft-compatible mouse; headphones or speakers.
500	__	$a Title from disc label.
520	__	$a Presents the complete Funk & Wagnalls new encyclopedia plus assorted sounds, music, spoken text, animation, illustrations, photographs, maps, and additional printed material. Features include topic tracker, hypertext category browser, bookmark and note functions, and interactive atlas and timeline. Most textual and visual material can be enlarged, copied, and printed for creating reports.
650	_0	$a Electronic encyclopedias.
710	2_	$a Microsoft Corporation.
730	02	$a Funk & Wagnalls new encyclopedia.
753	__	$a Multimedia PC $c MS-DOS 3.1
753	__	$a CD-ROM drive

of materials except for "text." The GMD should appear in square brackets immediately following the title proper, since its purpose is to identify the class of material to which an item belongs and to distinguish between different forms of the same work at an early stage in the description. It precedes any other title information, such as a subtitle. Use of the GMD "text" is optional. Most agencies do not use it for books, since library users normally assume that the record describes a book.

Notes

AACR2R provides for many optional elements. The note area of the catalog record has probably the widest range of options. Notes may be provided if deemed important by the cataloging agency, or they may be accepted as part of a record from a vendor.

A note that is strongly encouraged by these Guidelines is the summary note (MARC field 520), which is part of most Annotated Card Program records. It consists of an objective statement of the most important elements of the plot, theme, or topic of the work. It should describe the unique aspects of the work and generally justify, whenever possible, the assigned subject headings, but it should not praise or criticize the item's content nor be so vague as to be useless. Words in the summary should be chosen to facilitate keyword searching in online catalogs. The use of synonyms for words found in the title and subject headings is helpful. Users of nonbook items are especially dependent on summary notes because of the limitations on browsing such materials.

A summary note is not required if a contents note (MARC field 505) that is descriptive of the nature and the scope of the work is used. A contents note may record the titles of individual selections contained on a sound recording or of programs on a videorecording.

Information about system requirements should be provided for sound recordings, videorecordings, and computer files (MARC field 538, System details note).

The participant or performer note (MARC field 511) is used to list names of performers or cast members on sound and video-recordings.

Two other notes are especially applicable to juvenile materials. The target audience note (MARC field 521) contains information about reading grade level, interest age level, or interest grade level of the intended audience of an item. The awards note (MARC field

586) contains information about awards, such as the Newbery Medal, that are associated with an item.

AACR2R implies the order in which notes are to be given. The summary note or the contents note is normally the last note. If both are present, the contents note should be last.

ISBN

The International Standard Book Number (ISBN) (MARC field 020) is required when available. The area for standard number and terms of availability (price) follows the area for notes on cards.

Name, Title, and Series Access Points

There is no variation from AACR2R in either choice or form of main entry for children's materials. The form of added entries for names and titles also remains the same. (For names used as subject access points, follow the Guidelines under Subject Headings.) The choice of added entries for names and titles, and the choice and form of series added entries are discussed below.

Name Access Points

Added entries for persons (MARC field 700) and corporate bodies (MARC field 710) are made to provide access to bibliographic records in addition to the access from the main entry heading.

1. Added entries should be made for all joint authors if two or three persons or bodies collaborated on the work. If four or more collaborated, only the first-named is traced.

2. Added entries for illustrators are required, as their contribution to a work may equal or overshadow that of a writer, and access to the illustrator is important not only for the artistic content but also for collocating works of historically important artists. Added entries are optional, however, for illustrators whose contribution consists only of cover, frontispiece, or insignificant or repeating chapter-head decorations, or for a designer who is not also the illustrator, such as a design studio. A separate added entry for an illustrator who is also the author is not necessary.

3. Added entries should be made for principal performers on sound recordings and for producers, directors, etc. for videorecordings unless there are more than three of each. If there are more than three, make an added entry under the one named first.

4. Although AACR2R allows the optional use of function designations for editors, compilers, etc. (subfield e of MARC field 700), only the designation "ill." (for illustrator) is required by these Guidelines.

Title Access Points

Do not apply all of the restrictions in AACR2R on tracing the title of an item entered under a personal heading, corporate heading, or uniform title (Rule 21.30J1). Follow these rules instead:

1. Trace the title even if the title proper is the same as an assigned subject heading or its direct reference. For younger users of a catalog, even a catalog in which name-title and subject entries are interfiled, this added access is important. It is essential for divided catalogs and also for online catalogs, in which the title must appear in the title index to allow for searching by title.
2. Trace the title even if the title proper is the same as the main entry heading for a personal or corporate name. It is not necessary to trace the title if the title proper is the same as a uniform title main entry heading.

In MARC records a first indicator of "1" in field 245 indicates that the title proper should be traced. Added entries should also be made for other versions of a title under which users are likely to search. Varying forms of titles are recorded in MARC field 246.

Series Access Points

Make a series added entry for each work in the series that is cataloged if it provides a useful access point. Add the number of the individual work within the series if there is a number. The series added entry may be traced the same as the series statement or it may be traced differently if the series statement varies from the established form of the series. In MARC bibliographic records a series that is traced the same is recorded in field 440. If the series is traced differently, the series statement is recorded in field 490 with a first indicator of "1" and the series added entry is recorded in an 8XX field.

Series access is particularly important for children's materials since the series is a source of information about the content and approach of a work.

Subject Headings

The primary source for subject headings is the most recent edition of the *Library of Congress Subject Headings* (LCSH) and the list of Annotated Card (AC) headings. The AC list was created to offer more appropriate subject headings for juvenile works and to afford easier subject access to the materials. Any heading chosen from LCSH should be checked against the list of AC headings to determine if it provides an exception to the LC heading. The list of AC headings appears in a separate section of the printed and microfiche versions of LCSH. Library of Congress Subject Headings are also available in electronic versions that are more current than the printed edition. AC records contained on the MARC Distribution Service subject authority weekly file may be identified by a value of "b" in field 008 position 11. Subject headings (both LC and AC) used on records for juvenile materials created by LC from 1983 to 1993 are listed in *Subject Headings for Children.*

Annotated Card headings are identified in Cataloging in Publication and on LC printed cards by brackets. Print programs may be modified to delete or keep the brackets as required by the individual library. In MARC bibliographic records, a second indicator of "1" in 6XX fields identifies AC headings or indicates that the formulation of the subject added entry conforms to AC practice. Any subject heading that does not conform to AC practice must either be coded to indicate its source (using the 6XX field second indicator) or entered in a local subject access field (69X). This would apply to subject headings from *Sears List of Subject Headings* if added by a vendor or local cataloging agency.

Special AC Application of Subject Headings

Some AC headings are simplified forms of standard LC headings, but the chief differences between AC and LC headings are in the AC rules for application of subject headings, summarized below.

1. Omission of the subdivision —**Juvenile literature** and related subdivisions such as —**Juvenile films**, and avoidance of special juvenile form headings (**Children's poetry**; **Children's plays**). (Words that would be superfluous in a juvenile catalog are deleted in topical headings. For example, **Parties** is used instead of **Children's parties**.)

2. Assignment of subject headings to fiction as well as nonfiction

to bring out the most important aspects of the work. The subdivision —**Fiction** is used when appropriate for subject headings applied to fictional material.

3. Assignment of both general and specific headings (e.g., **Turtles** and **Sea turtles**) to a work if both provide useful subject access.

4. Provision of headings designating form (e.g., **Jokes**; **Stories in rhyme**) whenever access by form of material appears helpful.

5. Use of both popular and scientific terms (e.g., **Cats** and **Felidae**), even for the same work, depending on whether the material is intended for very young and/or older children. (Note, however, that the AC list customarily substitutes the common names of animals and plants for the scientific ones in the LC standard list.)

Creation of New Subject Headings

If the AC list and LCSH do not provide suitable terminology for the children's materials at hand, the following steps may be taken:

1. Modify LC subject headings to modernize spelling and to anglicize foreign names.

2. Refer to other established subject heading lists, such as *Sears List of Subject Headings,* for headings not found in LCSH.

Use of the 658 Field for Curricular Objectives

If it is deemed important to list index terms denoting curriculum or course-study objectives applicable to the materials being described, use standard published sources and identify the source in subfield $2 of the 658 field.

Classification

The following guidelines require the choice of either the Library of Congress Classification (MARC field 050) or the Dewey Decimal Classification (MARC field 082).

Library of Congress Classification

1. For fiction, assign numbers from the PZ schedule.

2. For nonfiction materials, assign numbers from the appropriate nonfiction schedule.

Dewey Decimal Classification

1. For fiction for preschool through second grade (K–2) or through age 8, assign the letter "E."

2. For fiction for third grade (age 9) and up, assign the abbreviation "Fic." (In the first edition of these guidelines, grade 3 was included in "E" collections. The policy limiting "E" to materials for users through grade 2 was implemented at the Library of Congress in August 1994.)

3. For biography, any of the following practices is appropriate:

   a. The letter "B" for any individual biography,
   b. The number "92" for individual biography and "920" for collective biography, or
   c. The class number representing the subject of the person's most noted contribution, as instructed in the current abridged edition of the Dewey Decimal Classification.

4. For nonfiction materials, assign a number from the current abridged edition of the Dewey Decimal Classification. Options for treatment of biography are described in item 3, above.

Classification of Folklore

Under either Library of Congress or Dewey classification, use these guidelines to determine whether or not an item is folklore:

1. Folklore is defined as those items of culture that are learned orally, by imitation or by observation, including narratives (tales, legends, proverbs, etc.). A story about fairies is not folklore unless it meets the criterion of having been handed down orally from generation to generation. It may be a modern piece of fantasy fiction instead.

2. Regard relatively faithful retellings and adaptations of folk material as folklore.

3. Do not consider religious mythology, stories from the Bible or other religious scriptures, modern fantasies, or drastic alterations of folk material as folklore, but class them elsewhere.

Local Implementation

Adopting this standard does not require libraries or catalogers to use records created by the Library of Congress or to accept all elements of records available online or through commercial vendors. Data manipulation and design of local card profiles are accommodated by most machine-readable formats and are provided by most commercial vendors and utilities. But libraries that contribute to shared databases and vendors who supply MARC records are expected to conform to standards. Libraries that do not use computer services now may well do so in the future. It is thus to the advantage of all libraries to have a recommended standard for cataloging juvenile materials. As a further benefit, by making children's cataloging compatible with that for adult materials—without sacrificing its unique characteristics—this standard enables the young user to understand the adult catalog.

The above-stated Guidelines give sufficient latitude for the individual cataloger or library to meet local needs while remaining within the standard. The recommendations in these Guidelines are intended to meet the requirements of young library users, in accordance with the purpose of the catalog record.

Sources for Consultation

It is recommended that the latest edition of the following professional tools be used in the application of these standards:

Abridged Dewey Decimal Classification and Relative Index. Albany, N.Y.: Forest Press.

Anglo-American Cataloguing Rules, 2d ed., 1988 rev., with Amendments 1993. Chicago: American Library Association.

Interactive Multimedia Guidelines Review Task Force. *Guidelines for Bibliographic Description of Interactive Multimedia.* Chicago: American Library Association.

Library of Congress. Cataloging Policy and Support Office. *Library of Congress Classification Schedules.* Washington, D.C.: Library of Congress.

Library of Congress. Cataloging Policy and Support Office. *Library of Congress Subject Headings.* Washington, D.C.: Library of Congress.

Library of Congress. Cataloging Policy and Support Office. *Subject Cataloging Manual: Subject Headings.* Washington, D.C.: Library of Congress.

Library of Congress. Network Development and MARC Standards Office. *USMARC Format for Bibliographic Data.* Washington, D.C.: Library of Congress.

Library of Congress. Office for Descriptive Cataloging Policy. *Library of Congress Rule Interpretations.* Washington, D.C.: Library of Congress.

McCroskey, Marilyn. *Cataloging Nonbook Materials with AACR2R and MARC: A Guide for the School Library Media Specialist.* Chicago: American Association of School Librarians, 1994.

Rose, Lois Doman, and Winifred E. Duncan. "LC's National Standard for Cataloging Children's Materials." *School Library Journal* 22, no. 5 (January 1976): 20–23.

Sears List of Subject Headings. New York: H. W. Wilson.

Subcommittee on Subject Access to Individual Works of Fiction, Drama, etc. *Guidelines on Subject Access to Individual Works of Fiction, Drama, Etc.* Chicago: American Library Association, 1990.

Subject Headings for Children. Edited by Lois Winkel. Albany, N.Y.: Forest Press, 1994.

2

The Annotated Card Program

Jane E. Gilchrist

MANY LIBRARIANS WORKING with children's collections in school and public libraries are surprised to learn that the Library of Congress provides subject cataloging designed especially for them and has been doing so since the fall of 1965. The Library's Annotated Card (AC) Program provides a more appropriate subject analysis of juvenile titles and offers easier subject access to the materials than standard Library of Congress cataloging.

The early 1960s were marked by increased interest in juvenile materials held by the Library of Congress. After hearing from patrons and card customers, the Library concluded there was a need for a modified catalog record that would be more suitable for libraries serving children and young adults. The Children's Literature Cataloging Office was established in November 1965 and was responsible for adapting cataloging done for the Library's general card catalog for use in juvenile catalogs. This special cataloging program was called the Annotated Card Program and was to concentrate on preparing records for currently issued children's literature and, time permitting, adapting existing LC records for juvenile titles that were still in print.

During the first two years of the Annotated Card Program, the AC record, which retained the standard descriptive cataloging but contained several additional elements that made the record more useful, was printed as a separate record and was assigned a unique card number with an AC prefix. Beginning in 1969, the Library decided to combine LC and AC records and issue one record made up of both standard Library of Congress cataloging and the special elements of the AC cataloging. The new card had an AC suffix as part of the card number. That numbering continues today. The subject headings assigned through the AC Program were bracketed on the combined card.

Shortly after the beginning of the AC Program, the library community became involved with the Library of Congress effort. In 1968, the American Library Association (ALA) formed an ad hoc committee to examine the cataloging needs of children's materials. The Committee on the Cataloging of Children's Materials began to study such questions as the cost of original cataloging done on the local level and the effect that developments in computer science might have on technical services and shared cataloging efforts. By 1969, the Committee concluded that after several desirable changes were made, LC's AC cataloging should be designated as the national standard for the cataloging of children's materials. Eventually this Committee produced guidelines for applying the recommended standard. A document entitled "Guidelines for Standardized Cataloging of Children's Materials" was published in *Top of the News* (Fall 1983). It described the bibliographic elements that were part of the standard AC record.

The most current version of the Guidelines, which appears elsewhere in this publication, can be used along with the *Anglo-American Cataloguing Rules,* second edition, 1988 revision, and the interpretations of them by the Library of Congress; *Library of Congress Subject Headings* (LCSH), current edition (including the Annotated Card Program list of subject headings); Dewey Decimal Classification or Library of Congress Classification; and the introduction to the Annotated Card Program, which appears in the introduction to the current edition of LCSH, to help those who find it necessary to do original AC cataloging for material in their collections and wish to conform to the standard.

The Committee, now a permanent part of the Association for Library Collections and Technical Services (ALCTS), continues to monitor the cataloging of children's materials and address cataloging issues that affect children's and young adult collections.

Today, the AC Program functions much as it did after the one-card record was instituted. The program is administered by the Children's Literature Team, which is part of the History and

Literature Cataloging Division of LC's Library Services. Partly because of the Cataloging in Publication (CIP) Program and the ever-growing MARC database, AC cataloging is readily available. Approximately 75 percent of the books receiving AC cataloging are part of the CIP Program and all AC records are added to the MARC database. On printed cards AC headings still appear in brackets. On a MARC record, the headings are identified by the second indicator of 1 in the 6XX field. Many vendors offer AC cataloging as one of the cataloging options.

AC Cataloging

Although the standard bibliographic record provides abundant information about the title it represents, the Annotated Card Program record includes several additional elements that are particularly useful in catalogs for children's and young adult collections. Added entries are always provided for title access and for all illustrators because of the importance of pictorial matter in juvenile works. Except for those receiving a descriptive contents note, most works receive a brief, noncritical annotation prepared by the AC cataloger. This annotation describes the work's scope and contents.

Until 1970, the AC Program provided an abridged Dewey number in addition to a Library of Congress Classification number for all works cataloged in the program. This included the [E] and [FIC] for belles lettres material. These designations were provided because many juvenile collections were arranged by the Dewey Decimal Classification system. Since 1970, the Decimal Classification Division has assumed responsibility for assigning unabridged Dewey numbers to AC records. The AC Program, however, continues to assign bracketed Dewey numbers to material the Decimal Classification Division deems out of scope.

The last element added to the AC record is a set of subject headings. Catalogers are free to use any valid Library of Congress subject heading and to establish additional headings that are valid only as Annotated Card Program headings. AC headings are established after consulting other subject heading lists, such as Sears and standard children's reference sources. Catalogers also apply intuition and common sense when documentation is not available. The AC headings fall into two categories, modified LC headings and new unique terms. LC headings are modified to update spelling, to anglicize foreign names, and to remove words or phrases that are superfluous in a juvenile catalog. Unique terms are those that do not appear in any list but are deemed appropriate for the juvenile catalog. The brief list of AC headings and an overview of the policies and practices of AC cataloging are published with the main list of LC subject headings in the microfiche and paper editions of LCSH. They are also available as part of the machine-readable version of LCSH.

From the beginning of the program, the chief difference between the AC and LC subject analysis has been in application rather than in form (see Figure 1). Certain subdivisions such as **—Juvenile literature** and **—Juvenile fiction** are deemed superfluous in a children's catalog and are routinely dropped. The use of the subdivision **—United States** is restricted to special cases because most of the material purchased by children's libraries in the United States reflects an American rather than an international orientation. For certain types of headings, all geographic subdivisions are omitted.

Unlike adult belles lettres material, juvenile belles lettres materials, including picture books, easy readers, and young adult novels, are given full subject analysis (see Figure 2). Subject headings for readily identifiable topics as well as abstract concepts are assigned because it is felt that such headings provide a useful approach to an important part of a library's collection.

Figure 1. Combined LC and AC Records, with Bracketed
AC Subject Headings

Giblin, James.
　　George Washington : a picture book biography / by James Cross Giblin ; illustrated by Michael Dooling. — New York : Scholastic, c1992.
　　　48 p. : col. ill., map ; 29 cm.
　　　Includes index.
　　　Summary: Examines the family life and career of the first American president, also discussing myths and legends, monuments to Washington, and Mount Vernon.
　　　ISBN 0-590-42550-1 : $14.95 (Higher in Canada)
　　　1. Washington, George, 1732-1799—Juvenile literature.　2. Presidents—United States—Biography—Juvenile literature.　₁1. Washington, George, 1732-1799.　2. Presidents₎　I. Dooling, Michael, ill.　II. Title.

E312.66.G53　1992　　　　　973.4'1'092—dc20　91-16614
　　　　　　　　　　　　　　　　₁B₎　　　　　AACR 2　MARC

　　Library of Congress　　　　　₁9508₎　　　　　　　AC

Figure 2. Juvenile Belles Lettres Material with Full Subject Analysis

---

Christian, Mary Blount.
    Sebastian (Super Sleuth) and the copycat crime / Mary Blount
Christian ; illustrated by Lisa McCue. — 1st ed. — New York
: Macmillan ; Toronto : Maxwell Macmillan Canada ; New York
: Maxwell Macmillan International, c1993.
     62 p. : ill. ; 21 cm.
    Summary: While speaking at a crime writers conference, bumbling detective
John Quincy Jones is aided by his capable canine in solving the mystery of two
missing manuscripts.
    ISBN 0-02-718211-8 : $11.95 ($14.95 Can.)

    ₁1. Mystery and detective stories. 2. Dogs—Fiction. 3. Authors—Fiction₁
I. McCue, Lisa, ill. II. Title.

PZ7.C4528 Scu   1993   ₁Fic₁—dc20   93-7038
                                            AACR 2 MARC

Library of Congress   AC

AC cataloging policy deviates slightly from LC policy by permitting the cataloger to assign both specific and general subject headings to the same work. It is also permissible to assign both popular and scientific terms.

The last major difference is the use of headings to denote form or kind. Assigning form headings, such as **Jokes**, **Stories without words**, and **Bible stories**, makes the material more accessible.

Since its inception, the AC Program has attempted to provide bibliographic records that would be useful in children's and young adult catalogs. To ensure this, the scope of the program, the cataloging policies, and the completed records are under constant review. The program actively seeks the opinions of librarians and others using AC cataloging and attempts to accommodate their suggestions. One of the biggest problems remains that of visibility. Libraries sometimes use AC cataloging without knowing its source. It is hoped that this chapter has provided information about the program and how it can be used. Further questions about the program and the construction and use of AC headings should be sent to:

      Annotated Card Program
      History and Literature Cataloging Division
      Library of Congress
      Washington, DC 20540

Bibliography

"Annotated Card Program: AC Subject Headings." In *Library of Congress Subject Headings,* 19th ed., xix–xxxvi. Washington, D.C.: Library of Congress. Cataloging Policy and Support Division, 1996.

Applebaum, Edmond L. "Library of Congress Annotated Cards for Children's Literature." *Library Resources & Technical Services* 10 (Fall 1966): 455–457.

"Guidelines for Standardized Cataloging of Children's Materials." *Top of the News* (Fall 1983): 49–55.

Hines, Patricia S. "Addendum to Article on Library of Congress Annotated Cards for Children's Literature." *Library Resources & Technical Services* 10 (Fall 1966): 457–460.

Rose, Lois Doman. "LC's National Standard for Cataloging Children's Materials: Explanation." *School Library Journal* 22, no. 5 (January 1976): 20–22.

Turner, Treva. "Cataloging Children's Materials at the Library of Congress." *Quarterly Journal of the Library of Congress* 30 (1973): 152–157.

3

Vendors of Cataloging for Children's Materials

Betty Vandivier

LIBRARIES PURCHASE CATALOGING in order to save time or money or both. Another goal of the small library with no cataloging specialists is to improve the quality and consistency of cataloging. Unless vendors and cataloging options are selected with care, however, the purchased product may not fit comfortably into the existing library catalog, thus causing frustration for staff and patrons alike.

Finding Sources of Cataloging

Librarians often become aware of vendors through journal advertisements and conference exhibits. However, it is difficult to quickly identify all the companies that supply cataloging records. An annual directory of suppliers of commercial cataloging is "Sourcebook: The Reference for Library Products & Services," published each December as a supplement to *Library Journal.* The "1996 Sourcebook" lists 17 companies under the heading "Book Catalog Services"; 10 companies under "Book Processing Kits"; 11 companies under "Cards, Catalog—Printed"; 29 companies under "Cataloging Services—Audiovisual Materials"; and 30 companies under "Cataloging Services—Books."[1] In each category, these totals reflect a steady increase in the numbers of cataloging services in the five-year period since *Library Journal*'s 1991 list.

Standard textbooks on cataloging concentrate primarily on original cataloging. Purchased cataloging, if mentioned at all, is most often discussed briefly and in a very general manner.[2] Direct comparisons of the options offered by the various vendors appear infrequently in the literature. The seventh edition of *Akers' Simple Library Cataloging,* published in 1984, features a comparison of eight suppliers of printed catalog cards that includes reproductions of catalog cards from those vendors.[3]

The lists of vendors at the end of this chapter were compiled from all the preceding sources. Companies that offer indexing services only or are self-described as serving "academic, research, and special libraries" were omitted.[4] Also outside the scope of this chapter are companies that sell computer software designed to assist libraries in the cataloging of materials, or software for reproduction of cataloging copy. Vendors of machine-readable cataloging, including CD-ROMs of MARC records, and suppliers of retrospective conversion services will be discussed in the chapter titled "Automating the Children's Catalog."

Characteristics of Cataloging Vendors

Many suppliers of commercial cataloging provide cataloging for books. Fewer suppliers provide cataloging for audiovisual materials. Vendors may provide cataloging for some audiovisual formats (e.g., sound recordings and computer software) but not others (e.g., film-strips and kits).

Some vendors supply cataloging for any item in their database while others provide cataloging only for books or audiovisual titles listed in their current catalog or purchased through their company.

Cataloging is available from several types of suppliers. Each U.S. company included in the list at the end of this chapter was listed or advertised in current buyers' guides and journals. Canadian companies listed were identified by Jean Weihs. Companies providing cataloging fall into these categories:

1. *Wholesalers:* There are hundreds of book and audiovisual wholesalers in the United States and Canada.[5] Most of them offer cataloging products or services or both for the books and audiovisual materials they sell.

2. *Vendors of prebound books:* Because many libraries prefer to buy prebound trade and paperback books, companies that sell cataloging services with prebound books bought through them are also listed.

3. *Cataloging vendors:* Some companies offer an array of cataloging products and services not tied to purchase of either books or audiovisual media.

4. *Bibliographic utilities:* Some of the organizations listed originated as not-for-profit bibliographic utilities. They were established by and for libraries and use computer databases of cataloging records contributed by user libraries and by national agencies. Libraries using the services of these companies sign a membership agreement. Most small public and school libraries using OCLC participate through membership in one of their locally governed regional networks, such as AMIGOS or SOLINET.[6]

5. *Publishers:* Though they are not listed at the end of the chapter, many individual publishers offer cataloging with their books and audiovisual items. These publishers generally purchase cataloging from other vendors rather than produce it themselves.

Considerations in Selecting a Cataloging Vendor

Before selecting a vendor, librarians may wish to consult the "Checklist for Commercial Processing Services," prepared in 1979 by the Commercial Technical Services Committee, a subcommittee of the former Resources and Technical Services Division (RTSD) of the American Library Association.[7] The subcommittee studied commercial processing services that provide bibliographic products in a variety of formats. The following discussion is based, in part, on the topics noted in the checklist. The checklist itself is too lengthy to reproduce here.[8]

Products Offered

One major consideration in selecting a vendor is the availability of a particular cataloging product or service. Vendors may offer such products as catalog cards; catalog card kits, including pockets, circulation cards, and labels; computer output microform (COM); bar codes and diskettes or magnetic tapes of MARC records for computer catalogs; and computer software for cataloging or card production. Services may include: providing shelf-ready books complete with spine labels, protective clear jackets, date due slips, checkout cards, and pockets; and special ordering and report features. Some vendors keep computerized records of all the materials a library purchases and can provide magnetic tapes or diskettes of the cataloging for those materials when a library decides to automate.

Order Procedures

In addition to looking at the products and services offered by a vendor, the librarian should carefully examine each vendor's order procedures. The amount of information required by each vendor and the form in which each vendor will accept orders may vary considerably. The librarian should select a commercial vendor that has ordering procedures compatible with those of the library. Selecting a vendor who can accept orders with a minimum of information per item may save the library a considerable amount of time in order preparation. The librarian should also note whether vendor requirements for handling returns and exchanges, invoices, and shipping are compatible with library procedures.

Profile Options and Cataloging Standards

The profile options a company offers are very important in making it possible to blend purchased cataloging successfully into the local catalog. The first time catalog cards or services are ordered from a particular vendor, the librarian will usually fill out a profile sheet indicating options selected by the library. The profile sheet remains on file with the vendor and need not be resubmitted unless a change of options is desired. Each order is simply submitted; no overall contract is required.

Taylor's *Cataloging with Copy: A Decision-Maker's Handbook* provides the most complete discussion of the problems and processes involved in integrating outside cataloging copy into the library's catalog.[9] A brief discussion is also presented in Miller and Terwillegar, *Commonsense Cataloging: A Cataloger's Manual,* which contains a helpful chapter titled, "Cataloging with Copy."[10] The following paragraphs discuss a number of cataloging elements that must be considered.

Bibliographic Description

Vendors may take descriptive cataloging content from several sources: Cataloging-in-Publication (CIP) data, machine-readable cataloging (MARC) records, or network copy (e.g., OCLC). If cataloging is not available through these sources, original cataloging may be done by the company's catalogers. Vendors may offer full descriptive cataloging, near copy (something close when the exact edition is not available), or a brief simplified description. Some companies provide annotations for children's materials. These annotations are often taken from Library of Congress Annotated Card Program cataloging records. All descriptive cataloging copy as well as the main and added entry headings should be prepared in accordance with the *Anglo-American Cataloguing Rules,* second edition, 1988 revision (AACR2R).

Subject Headings

Vendors may provide subject headings from *Sears List of Subject Headings* or the *Library of Congress Subject Headings.* If a library is using Library of Congress subject headings, the special juvenile subject headings provided by the Annotated Card Program of the Library of Congress should be selected for children's materials if they are offered as an option. It is helpful to note whether the vendor places a limit on the number of subject headings it will assign to a work.

Classification

Librarians also need to specify classification options. Library of Congress Classification, Dewey Decimal Classification, or both may be offered as classification options. If Dewey classification is used, note whether it is possible to specify use of the abridged or the unabridged edition. Other considerations for call numbers include whether Cutter numbers or author letters are used, and whether provisions are made for alternate symbols, such as B, 92, F, Fic, j, or E. Because changing classification numbers is time consuming, it is more efficient and effective to order from a vendor who can supply the options already in use in the library's collection. Some numbers may still need to be revised if the library does not change to new editions of the classification manuals as quickly as the cataloging service does (or vice versa).

Special Features

It may be possible to order additional main entry cards or extra shelflist cards. Sometimes a charge is made for these additional cards. A filing option available from some vendors allows a library to receive catalog cards arranged according to its needs. For example, instead of getting individual card sets for each book in an order, a library can receive the cards for an entire order already interfiled and ready to be placed in the public catalog, along with a separate group of shelflist cards arranged by classification number.[11] Vendors may also provide extra information on the shelflist or MARC record, such as readability or interest levels, curriculum connections, date purchased, review sources, and price. Libraries with an online public access catalog should be able to purchase only a shelflist card or no catalog cards.

Notes

1. "1996 Sourcebook: The Reference for Library Products & Services," Supplement to *Library Journal* (December 1995). Another readily available annual guide is a commercial publication: *The Librarian's Yellow Pages, '96* (Larchmont, N.Y.: Garance, 1996).

2. Cataloging texts consulted: Lois Mai Chan, *Cataloging and Classification: An Introduction,* 2d ed. (New York: McGraw-Hill, 1993); Susan Grey Akers, *Akers' Simple Library Cataloging,* 7th ed., completely revised and rewritten by Arthur Curley and Jana Varlejs (Metuchen, N.J.: Scarecrow Press, 1984); Arlene G. Taylor, *Cataloging with Copy: A Decision-Maker's Handbook,* 2d ed. (Englewood, Colo.: Libraries Unlimited, 1988); Mildred H. Downing, *Introduction to Cataloging and Classification,* 6th ed. (Jefferson, N.C.: McFarland, 1992); Rosalind Miller and Jane Terwillegar, *Commonsense Cataloging: A Cataloger's Manual,* 4th ed., rev. (New York: H. W. Wilson, 1990); and Bohdan S. Wynar, *Introduction to Cataloging and Classification,* 8th ed., edited by Arlene G. Taylor (Englewood, Colo.: Libraries Unlimited, 1992).

3. Akers, *Akers' Simple Library Cataloging,* 282–303.

4. The buying guides consulted typically provide company name, address, telephone and FAX numbers, and a brief paragraph describing services. *Library Journal*'s "1996 Sourcebook" also lists a contact name and e-mail address. Both the "Sourcebook" and *The Librarian's Yellow Pages* include some company advertisements.

5. *American Book Trade Directory 1995–1996,* 41st ed. (New York: R. R. Bowker, 1995).

6. Although they are part of OCLC, AMIGOS and SOLINET are also listed separately in the list because they have acquired non-OCLC software and to some extent compete with OCLC in several areas of cataloging for libraries. RLIN, another major bibliographic utility, is not listed, as it specializes in serving the needs of academic research institutions.

7. Subsequently renamed the Association for Library Collections and Technical Services (ALCTS).

8. Commercial Processing Services Committee, Resources and Technical Services Division, American Library Association, "Checklist for Commercial Processing Services," *Library Resources & Technical Services* 23 (Spring 1979): 177–182.

9. Taylor, *Cataloging with Copy.*

10. Miller and Terwillegar, *Commonsense Cataloging.*

11. This service is especially helpful for opening day collections for new libraries. Vendors also offer the service of shipping the collection boxed in shelflist order or near-shelflist order.

Vendors

Because the marketplace changes rapidly, specific product information is not provided for the vendors listed here. Librarians considering a change of vendor should write or telephone several vendors to get current information on product offerings and prices for comparison purposes.

U.S. and Canadian wholesalers that offer cataloging products with the purchase of books and audiovisual materials:

Baker & Taylor
2709 Water Ridge Parkway
Charlotte, NC 28217
(704) 357-3500
(800) 775-1800
FAX: (704) 329-8989
e-mail: BTinfo@baker-taylor.
     e-mail.com

Blackwell North America, Inc.
6024 SW Jean Road, Bldg G
Lake Oswego, OR 97035
(503) 684-1140
(800) 547-6426
FAX: (503) 639-2481
e-mail: bridges@bnamf.
     blackwell.com

Brodart, Inc.
500 Arch Street
Williamsport, PA 17705
(717) 326-2461
(800) 233-8467
FAX: (800) 999-6799
e-mail: salesmkt@brodard.com
http://www.brodart.com

John Coutts Library Services, Ltd.
6900 Kinsman Court
P.O. Box 1000
Niagara Falls, ON L2E 7E7
(905) 356-6382
(800) 263-1686
FAX: (905) 356-5064
e-mail: coutts@wizbang. coutts. on.ca
EDI installed

Follett Library Resources
4506 Northwest Highway
Crystal Lake, IL 60014-7393
(815) 455-1100
(800) 435-6170
FAX: (800) 852-5458
e-mail: custserv@flr.follett.com

Hispanic Books Distributors
1665 West Grant Road
Tucson, AZ 85745
(800) 634-2124

Ingram Library Services, Inc.
One Ingram Boulevard
La Vergne, TN 37086-1986
(800) 937-5300
FAX: (615) 793-3810

Lectorum Publications, Inc.
111 Eighth Avenue, Suite 804
New York, NY 10011-5201
(212) 929-2833
(800) 345-5946
FAX: (212) 727-3035

Shirley Lewis Information Services, Inc.
196 North Queen Street
Etobicoke, ON M9C 4Y1
(416) 622-3336
(800) 665-9464
FAX: (416) 622-0133
    (800) 668-2564
e-mail: slis@flexnet.com
http://www.shirleylewis.com
EDI installed

Library Services Center
141 Dearborn Place
Waterloo, ON N2J 4N5
(519) 746-4420
(800) 265-3360
FAX: (519) 746-4425
EDI installed

Mook & Blanchard
P.O. Box 1295
La Puente, CA 91749
(818) 968-6424
(800) 875-9911
FAX: (818) 968-6877

National Book Service
3269 American Drive
Mississauga, ON L4V 1V4
(905) 673-2644
(800) 387-3178
FAX: (905) 673-3365
    (800) 303-6697
e-mail: nbs@nbs.com

Professional Media Service Corp.
19122 S. Vermont Avenue
Gardena, CA 90248
(310) 532-9024
(800) 223-7672
FAX: (310) 532-0131
    (800) 253-8853
e-mail: promedia@class.org

S & B Books, Ltd.
3043 Universal Drive
Mississauga, ON L4X 2E2
(905) 629-5055
(800) 997-7099
FAX: (905) 629-5054
EDI installed

United Library Services
7140 Fairmount Drive SE
Calgary, AB T2H OX4
(403) 252-4426
FAX: (403) 258-3426

Companies that provide cataloging for prebound books purchased through them:

Bound to Stay Bound Books, Inc.
1880 West Morton Road
Jacksonville, IL 62650-2697
(217) 245-5191
(800) 637-6586
FAX: (800) 747-2872
e-mail: btsb@btsbooks.com

Demco Media
P.O. Box 14260
Madison, WI 53714-0260
(608) 241-1471
(800) 448-8939
FAX: (608) 241-0666
    (800) 828-0401

Econo-Clad Books
2101 N. Topeka Boulevard
P.O. Box 1777
Topeka, KS 66601
(913) 233-4252
(800) 255-3502
FAX: (913) 233-3129
    (800) 628-2410
e-mail: support@econoclad.com
http://www.econoclad.com

Library Bound, Inc.
200 Frobisher Drive
Waterloo, ON N2V 2A2
(519) 885-3233
(800) 363-4728
FAX: (519) 885-2662
e-mail: cpmlbi@nic.hookup.net

Perma-Bound Books
617 E. Vandalia Road
Jacksonville, IL 62650
(217) 243-5451
(800) 637-6581
FAX: (217) 243-7505
    (800) 551-1169

Companies offering a variety of cataloging products and services for books and some audiovisual formats, independent of their purchase:

Catalog Card Company
12221 Wood Lake Drive
Burnsville, MN 55337-1537
(612) 882-8558
(800) 328-2923
FAX: (612) 882-1504

Duncan Systems Specialists
700 Dorval Drive, Suite 605
Oakville, ON L6K 3W7
(905) 338-5545
(800) 836-5049
FAX: (905) 338-1847

Library Data Services
Box 1054
Stouffville, ON L4A 8A1
(905) 640-3716
FAX: (905) 640-3229
e-mail: caromori@enoreo.on.ca

Library of Congress
Cataloging Distribution
    Service
Washington, DC 20541-5017
(202) 707-6100
(800) 255-3666
FAX: (202) 707-1334
e-mail: cdsinfo@mail.loc.gov

London West Resource
    Centre
R.R. #2
Lambeth, ON N0L 1S5
(519) 471-4921
FAX: (519) 471-4921
EDI installed

Marcive, Inc.
P.O. Box 47508
San Antonio, TX 78265-7508
(210) 646-6161
(800) 531-7678
FAX: (210) 646-0167
e-mail: info@marcive.com

Organizations that began as bibliographic utilities and now offer a wide range of cataloging products and services to libraries:

AMIGOS Bibliographic Council, Inc.
1300 N. Central Expressway, #321
Dallas, TX 75243
(214) 750-6130

ISM Library Information Services
3300 Bloor Street West, 16th Floor, West Tower
Toronto, ON M8X 2X2
(416) 236-7171
(800) 268-0982
FAX: (416) 236-7541
http://www.ism.ca/lis

OCLC, Inc.
6565 Frantz Road
Dublin, OH 43017-3395
(614) 764-6000
(800) 848-5878
FAX: (614) 764-0155
http://www.oclc.org/

SOLINET
1438 W. Peachtree NW
Atlanta, GA 30309-2955
(404) 892-0943
(800) 999-8558
FAX: (404) 892-7879
e-mail: solinet_information@ soline

WLN
P.O. Box 3888
Lacey, WA 98509-3888
(360) 923-4000
(800) 342-5956
FAX: (360) 923-4009
e-mail: info@wln.com

4

How the CIP Program Helps Children's Librarians

Susan Vita

Revised by John Celli

C IP, OR CATALOGING IN PUBLICATION, is a cooperative program, begun in 1971, whose partners are the Library of Congress and approximately 4,000 participating members of the U.S. publishing industry. Publishers send galleys or front matter for their forthcoming books to the Library of Congress to have cataloging data prepared in advance of publication so that the data can be printed in the book.

The CIP program attempts to include materials that are heavily collected by U.S. libraries for which cataloging information is needed. Basically, this results in the inclusion of all monographs published in the United States. However, there are a few exceptions to this rule. Some of them are: consumable material, that is, material meant to be written in; material of a transitory nature, for example, cut-out books, calendars, and phone books; textbooks below the secondary school level; sheet music; mass-market paperbacks; religious instructional materials; self-published or subsidized books; and audiovisual materials. In FY96, CIP data were provided for approximately 51,000 titles.

Why Do Publishers Participate?

There are many answers to this question. Publishers want to make their books more attractive to their library customers. Generally, when a book arrives in a library it cannot circulate or be put on the shelf for browsing until a record is made. Books containing CIP data arrive with the intellectual work of cataloging already done, so that processing is simplified, and the books are available to the public sooner. Books published without CIP data require that someone on the library's staff produce the cataloging or that another library's cataloging record be found and copied or that the book be put aside in the hope that either LC or another library will catalog it.

Publishers also believe that the CIP program helps them sell more books. In addition to the CIP data appearing in the book, a machine-readable version of the record is created; this is known as MARC cataloging (MAchine-Readable Cataloging). These MARC CIP records are distributed to subscribers of the MARC tapes, and thus the word gets out to the library, library wholesaler, and bookstore markets that these books will soon be available. In short, CIP is another marketing tool for publishers.

How Does the CIP Program Help Children's Librarians?

A very high percentage of juvenile trade books is included in the CIP program. In FY96, 5,676 juvenile titles received CIP data. Library of Congress cataloging records are available for most juvenile books. Consequently, children's librarians who type their own cards have copy from which to prepare their cards as soon as the book arrives.

Libraries that purchase cataloging records from a commercial company can usually assume the cataloging they receive is based on LC cataloging. Libraries that are part of a library network, such as OCLC, and that produce their catalog records from a network database will locate CIP records when they search. In short, no matter what method a library uses to produce its catalog copy, the CIP program should save it time and money and improve the quality of its cataloging.

Because the CIP record is created from prepublication information supplied by the publisher, it must sometimes be changed after the published book is examined by a cataloger. The CIP record in the book is an abbreviated version of the LC prepublication catalog record. At the same time that it is supplied to the publisher for printing in the book, the full cataloging record appears on the MARC tapes. Publishers frequently report bibliographic changes before publication, so that both the CIP record in the book and the

MARC record can be updated. Any unreported changes are incorporated in the final MARC record, which is updated using the published book. This accounts for the differences that sometimes occur between the CIP data in the book or the information on the MARC record and the actual published book.

Other Ways That CIP Helps Children's Librarians

In addition to the time and resources saved in cataloging, the CIP Program provides other benefits. CIP data, for example, are often used in book selection. As noted earlier, at the same time the CIP record is sent to the publisher it is also distributed to subscribers of the MARC tapes. These subscribers are book vendors, publishers, and large library networks who, in turn, make the CIP records available in the products and services they provide.

The Library of Congress CDS Alert Service is one such service. CDS (Cataloging Distribution Service) gives subscribers the opportunity to choose books that interest them from among 2,155 subject categories, for example, picture books for children or children's literature. Subscribers then receive a CIP record weekly for each title that matches that subject interest. Some book vendors offer similar services, although it may not be immediately evident to the customer that the advance notice records of forthcoming titles are in fact CIP records.

Book vendors also use CIP records when selling books to libraries on approval. The CIP records on MARC tapes tell vendors what is being published and enable them to select and ship to libraries those titles that meet a prearranged selection criterion. Appearance of CIP records on the MARC tapes assures their inclusion in certain selection and review publications, and consequently brings their existence to the attention of children's librarians.

CIP records are also used in public services. The summaries that appear in CIP records for children's literature are especially valuable for public service and are consulted frequently to provide users an immediate brief description of the book's content. The summaries are also used in compiling bibliographies, in book talks, and, in combination with the subject headings, in locating other books on a similar topic.

The CIP program is a useful tool for children's librarians. Perhaps this description of its possible uses will inspire librarians to be more imaginative in looking for ways in which CIP can make their jobs easier and result in more effective service.

5

Using AACR2R in Cataloging Children's Collections

Sharon Zuiderveld

T HE CHILDREN'S LIBRARIAN in a school media center or public library is faced with many challenges, not least of which is how to maintain consistently high cataloging standards for the collection he or she maintains. Having concise, accurate, and consistent cataloging of all materials is even more important as schools and public libraries form consortia, join networks, and develop union lists to assist in collection development. It is important to be knowledgeable about cataloging in order to properly establish and maintain a card or online catalog for students, teachers, and administrators. A brief introduction to current cataloging rules and practices follows.

Whether derived cataloging comes from a bibliographic utility, from a commercial vendor, or directly from the Library of Congress, all these sources use the same set of rules to guide them in making decisions about the choice and form of headings and bibliographic description of items. The AACR2R Rules are used not only in many countries but in numerous languages. A committee of librarians from the United Kingdom, Australia, Canada, and the United States meets regularly to discuss additions or corrections to the rules, thus assuring catalogers that new types of items or new rule interpretations from the Library of Congress are incorporated into the latest edition of the code.

The code is divided into two main sections: rules governing the description of items to be cataloged and rules establishing the choice and form of headings for different parts of the description.

Realizing that not all libraries require that items in their collections be described to the same extent, AACR2R defines three levels of description, although the second level is most commonly used by the Library of Congress and standard cataloging agencies. The level a library uses should be based on the purpose of the catalog, however. For instance, a library with a large concentration of folklore may wish to catalog those items more fully than the other items in the collection. By the same token, a library containing vast audiovisual resources for curriculum enhancement may wish to catalog those items in greater detail.

The first level, brief cataloging, requires recording only the author, title, edition statement, publisher's name and date of publication, a brief physical description, notes essential to the use of an item, and standard numbers (ISBN and ISSN) (see Figure 1). The second level adds all relevant statements of responsibility, place of publication, all pertinent items in the physical description, any series statements, and notes of an informational nature (see Figure 2). The second level is recommended by the latest edition of the Guidelines for Standardized Cataloging of Children's Materials, included in this volume, and the Library of Congress. The third level includes everything called for by the rules applicable to the item being cataloged; this level is frequently used in academic and research libraries. The rules were designed so that libraries could interfile all levels within one collection. Although the first level must include the minimum elements, other elements may be added if needed for the patrons to be served. In children's collections, for instance, a series statement can be added to the first level if it is

Figure 1.   First-Level Description

Simon, Seymour.
    The heart.—Morrow Junior Books,
c1996.
    unp.

ISBN: 0-688-11407-5

I. Title.

Figure 2. Second-Level Description

Simon, Seymour.
    The heart : our circulatory system / Seymour
Simon.—New York : Morrow Junior Books,
c1996.
    unp. : col. ill. ; 27 cm.

    SUMMARY: Describes the heart, blood, and
other parts of the body's circulatory system and
explains how each component functions.

ISBN: 0-688-11407-5

I. Title.

considered important in locating material for a class or unit of study. Once a level of description has been selected, one must not feel rigidly bound to include only those elements in each record. The Guidelines for Standardized Cataloging of Children's Materials recommend use of the second level, in order to include dimensions, other statements of responsibility (such as illustrator or joint author), and series, these items being considered essential as searching tools in children's collections.

Another feature making AACR2R valuable to catalogers of children's collections is that the rules are based on principles applicable to all types of library materials, both book and nonbook. Separate chapters are devoted to the particular elements unique to sound recordings, motion pictures, videorecordings, maps, realia, and computer files.

A third feature making AACR2R accessible to those who work with children's collections is the Cataloging in Publication (CIP) program, begun in 1971 by the Library of Congress and 27 publishers. Currently, over 4,000 publishers participate in the CIP program. Publishers send galley proofs or title pages and front matter (such as introductions and tables of contents) to the Library of Congress to have cataloging data prepared in advance so that they can appear in the book when it is published. (See the chapter titled "How the CIP Program Helps Children's Librarians" in this volume.) Because an automated MARC (MAchine-Readable Cataloging) record is also created for each CIP record, libraries with access to bibliographic databases can locate these records quickly and usually save time and money while improving the quality of cataloging. Use of AACR2R in the CIP record assures the cataloger that current cataloging practices have been followed for descriptive cataloging and choice and form of headings.

For those unfamiliar with the acronym MARC, it simply refers to the fact that all the items on a catalog card are placed in a format that can be "read" by a computer. (A more thorough explanation appears in the chapter on MARC in this volume.) Thus, main entries, titles, pagination, and subject headings, to name a few of the most obvious items in a catalog record, are assigned specific tags or fields in a MARC record that can be called up on a computer screen. Although the format on the screen often looks quite different from the familiar catalog card, all the essential information about a particular item is contained within the record and is easily retrievable by the cataloger. The Library of Congress, bibliographic utilities, commercial vendors of cards, and even software programs for producing your own catalog cards make use of MARC records.

Several aids are available for the busy practitioner. *Maxwell's Handbook for AACR2: Explaining and Illustrating the Anglo-American Cataloguing Rules and 1993 Amendments* by Robert Maxwell and Margaret F. Maxwell complements and further clarifies the rules as well as provides numerous examples. Michael Gorman's *Concise AACR2, 1988 Revision,* though not a true abridgment, was written to express the rules in a simple way. A fine pamphlet for the beginner, *MARC Records,* originally written by Betty Furrie, is currently available from the Library of Congress. It provides numerous examples of book and nonbook records in the MARC format, following the rules established by AACR2R. The *Anglo-American Cataloguing Rules,* 2d edition, 1988 revision and 1993 Amendments will soon be available in a CD-ROM format for Windows 3.X through the American Library Association.

For both the novice and the experienced cataloger, the *Anglo-American Cataloguing Rules* provides a clear, well-defined set of rules to follow when cataloging items to be placed in a collection. As questions arise about cataloging and as new formats emerge, the committee members representing the nations participating in formulating the rules continue to address these new needs and include them in rule revisions, assuring the practitioner that consistency and accuracy are maintained in all matters of cataloging.

Bibliography

Furrie, Betty. *Understanding MARC Bibliographic: Machine-Readable Cataloging.* 4th ed. Washington, D.C.: Library of Congress, Cataloging Distribution Service, 1994.

Gorman, Michael. *The Concise AACR2, 1988 Revision.* Chicago: American Library Association, 1989.

Maxwell, Robert, and Margaret F. Maxwell. *Maxwell's Handbook for AACR2R: Explaining and Illustrating the Anglo-American Cataloguing Rules and 1993 Amendments.* Chicago: American Library Association, 1997.

6

Authority Control

Ruth Bogan

COMPUTER," COMMANDS THE YOUNG ACTOR in the futuristic jumpsuit, "what makes those little Earth-bugs light up?" And before you can say "beam me up," a soothing voice delivers an age-appropriate explanation of bioluminescence in fireflies. Wondrous, and simple, and, for the time being, science fiction. How does a computer know that when its young friend says bugs he means fireflies, and that they go by any one of several names? Who taught the computer that glowing animals display bioluminescence? Who programmed its authority control?

Authority control, according to Doris Clack, is based on uniqueness, standardization, and linkages.[1] In other words, when catalogers assign name and subject headings to catalog records, they abide by three promises. They pledge to:

1. give unique names to people, bodies, objects, and concepts;

2. use the names they have chosen consistently, each time they refer to those people, bodies, objects, and concepts; and

3. identify other possible names for those people, bodies, objects, and concepts, connecting them to the chosen names.

If a cataloger decides that the best name for the glowing bugs is fireflies, he records that decision in a subject heading list or thesaurus, and assigns the subject heading **Fireflies** whenever he catalogs works about them. Another cataloger may recognize that people in the Midwest refer to fireflies as lightning bugs and that entomologists might call them lampyridae. Consequently, she links these other names to the heading **Fireflies**.

Authority control has two purposes. It is a means for catalogers to communicate with one another and, more important, to communicate with the people who use library catalogs. Catalogers inform one another of their decisions by means of special notations, for example, USE, UF, BT, in subject heading lists, thesauri, and authority files. They translate this shorthand notation into more understandable references, such as "See," "See also," "Search also under," and so on, in public catalogs.

Subject Authority Control

In practice, catalogers distinguish between subject authority control and authority control of names and titles. For subject headings catalogers rely on lists and thesauri, including *Sears List of Subject Headings* (Sears), *Library of Congress Subject Headings* (LCSH), and LC's Annotated Card (AC) Program subject headings. These lists supply unique headings and identify many alternative headings for use as cross-references.

A basic truth of subject authority control is that the closer the language of a subject heading list comes to matching the language of the catalog users, the less authority control is needed. *Language,* here, means both terminology and the rules of application. **Fireflies** is the preferred subject heading in the LCSH and AC lists. If some children call them lightning bugs, the cataloger needs to steer those children to the authorized heading. The traditional catalog card form of reference would be:

> Lightning bugs
>
> > SEE Fireflies

The form of the references is flexible. Online catalogs might display them differently, but the meaning is the same. Catalogers are free, of course, to add cross-references as needed. When the primary grade students insist fireflies are "lightning bugs," it would be wise to make the reference

> Lighting bugs
>
> > SEE Fireflies

The introductory chapter of the Sears list, "Principles of the Sears List of Subject Headings," contains an excellent explanation of how to make and record references and is good background even for those who do not use Sears.

Both LCSH and Sears instruct catalogers to use specific subject headings. If a book is about fireflies, the cataloger will assign the heading **Fireflies**. If young catalog users commonly begin a search more generally, then the catalog should also steer them from broader topics to more specific ones:

> Insects
>
> > Search also under
> >
> > > Fireflies

The Annotated Card Program bends the rules on specific entry and encourages catalogers to use broader subject headings in addition to specific ones in certain cases. This does not eliminate the need for references, but it does make authority control less of a concern.

Name Authority Control

Authority control extends to names as well as subjects. Names include personal names (authors, illustrators, editors), corporate names (companies, organizations), and geographic names. In general, catalogers impose the same three demands on names that they do on subjects: (1) uniqueness, (2) consistent use, and (3) cross-references to link different forms. Decisions about how names should appear in catalog records are recorded in a name authority file. Creating unique name headings, identifying variant names, and linking them all together can be a time-consuming process, so catalogers often rely on the Library of Congress name authority file for name headings. LC publishes its name authority file in several formats. Vendors of cataloging, online systems vendors, and utilities like OCLC may also provide access to the file. Librarians who outsource cataloging should know what name authority file is being used in their cataloging.

To create unique name headings for personal names, catalogers try to distinguish between two or more people with identical names. One way to do this is to add a date or qualifier to the name. If three women named Susan Jones happen to write a book or illustrate a story or play the piano, their name headings might be established as:

Jones, Susan, 1955–

Jones, Susan, 1961–

Jones, Susan, pianist

Keep in mind that a small collection may have only one Susan Jones in its catalog with no need to distinguish her from anyone else. The Library of Congress will likely have several. The prevailing wisdom is that LC's name headings are so widely used, catalogers will accept them even if dates and qualifiers are unnecessary. Consistency is what is important. If Susan Jones the illustrator is "Jones, Susan, 1961–" on some records in a catalog, she should be so on all records.

Finally, there is the matter of linking other forms of a name to the chosen form. Most names don't require references. Some need several. Women, for example, frequently change their names when they marry, and catalogers make references between the two forms. Compound surnames, because they may be searched several ways, also require cross-references.

Practicing Authority Control

There are many ways to practice authority control. Authority control can be internal or external to a catalog. Internal control is integrated into a search; a user is guided as she uses the catalog. External control is provided by aids outside the catalog. Authority control can extend to every heading in a catalog, or it can be applied selectively. In addition, the practical details of authority control differ depending on whether one works with a card catalog, an online catalog with authority control, or one without.

Card catalogs and online catalogs with integrated authority control modules allow internal control. In the card catalog this means the familiar typed or printed cross-reference cards. In online catalogs internal control is provided by MARC authority records. Like MARC bibliographic records, authority records contain MARC-encoded information about headings and cross-references that can be manipulated and displayed by the system into which they are loaded. LC's name and subject authority files and, just recently, the AC subject heading file are available in MARC format. Various vendors supply these and other MARC authority records. Often catalogers can find themselves too busy to keep up an integrated authority control system, whether in a card catalog or online public access catalog (OPAC). Some online systems simply cannot support internal control, and all authority control must be done externally. A librarian who is both familiar with the headings in the catalog and willing to help users is an external authority control system, and probably a pretty good one. A copy of the subject heading list (Sears or LCSH, for example) kept close to the public catalog for users also provides external control.

Not all headings need the same degree of attention. If time is short, reserve the internal control, the typed cards, and the cross-references for the most troublesome or most popular headings. Decide which names are most likely to be confusing or misspelled and provide references for those. "Which way," a young catalog user might wonder, "do I search?" Is it:

X, Malcolm	*or*	Malcolm X?
Princess Diana	*or*	Diana, Princess?
Banks, Lynne Reid	*or*	Reid Banks, Lynne?

In the end ingenious librarians who recognize the benefits of authority control come up with solutions, often in spite of the local limitations. One frustrated music cataloger, working with an uncontrolled OPAC, taped eye-catching notices to the public terminals reminding users how to spell Tchaikovsky. This is an example of selective, external, and certainly effective authority control.

Authority control would be considerably easier if the target would hold still. New name and subject headings are created, and established ones change regularly, threatening to throw the cataloger's pledge of consistency right out the window. Again, the solution differs with the catalog. In a card catalog outdated headings can be changed and cross-references adjusted. Minor heading changes can be interfiled. If correcting cards is out of the question—no time, no help, too many cards involved—the card catalog graciously accommodates a reference explaining the change and directing the user to the new heading for the latest materials. MARC authority records can be easier to edit. Best of all, some online systems have global change capabilities, which allow catalogers to correct large numbers of headings with a few keystrokes.

Even the most sophisticated information system requires authority control and always will. The responsibility may change but not the concept. Children today must deal with systems that provide good authority control (the library catalog, we hope), some control (the phone book), and little, if any, internal authority control (the Internet). The mind-reading computers of TV series are for the future, but good, thoughtful authority control is a welcome mat to the catalogs of today and a lesson in how information is gathered.

Note

1. Doris Hargrett Clack, *Authority Control: Principles, Applications, and Instructions* (Chicago: American Library Association, 1990).

Additional Source

Outsourcing Cataloging, Authority Work, and Physical Processing: A Checklist of Considerations (Chicago: American Library Association, 1995).

7

How Children Search

Lynne A. Jacobsen

U NDERSTANDING HOW CHILDREN search and retrieve library materials can greatly improve children's cataloging practices, influence interface design, and impact future technologies.

Studies show that the age and the developmental stage of children determine how well they can search. Children age 10 and under are still developing their cognitive abilities. They have not yet developed the ability to recall terms and concepts. Children at this stage are better at recognizing words when they see them. Also, these children have a smaller knowledge base and weak alphabetizing skills, and they do not yet apply logic to problem solving. These skills are necessary for successful searching. Children age 11 and up have more success searching because their cognitive abilities are further developed; however, they also experience difficulty at times because of gaps in their knowledge base.

Though children like computers, they frequently have trouble using online catalogs. First of all, the volume of information presented is overwhelming. With an online catalog, children often view both adult and juvenile materials. In some cases, children are viewing the holdings of other libraries as well. Children are unable to scan so much material to find what they want. They are unable to skip over what is in between what is desired. Children will take the time to read every entry, sounding out the words they don't know.

Children also have difficulty spelling words correctly, typing, spacing, and determining proper word order. Many online catalogs are very literal, meaning any error in spelling, spacing, or word order will retrieve nothing. Keyword searching provides some remedy, but usually the opposite problem occurs with too many hits and too many out-of-context hits. Children have difficulty sorting through these search results. Boolean searching and search limiters improve the precision of keyword searching, but these concepts are too complicated for children 10 and under.

Online catalogs require a series of steps for searching, which is problematic for children. They not only have trouble determining what to search, but they have trouble coming up with alternative strategies when a search is unsuccessful. Children use natural language with their queries, when a controlled vocabulary term, such as a Library of Congress subject heading, is required. The vocabulary of many Library of Congress subject headings requires knowledge of terms that are above the sixth grade reading level. "Focus group data showed that children would rather not use any library catalog. They prefer to go directly to the shelves to find books. If that doesn't work, they will ask a friend or a librarian. They turn to a catalog only if all other strategies fail."[1]

At the Denver Public Library, a study showed that only 29 percent of searches by third, fourth, and fifth grade students were successful using CARL and NOTIS online catalogs. The problems were attributed to the following areas: "catalog mechanics (21.2%), bibliographic knowledge (18.4%), unsuccessful search strategy (11.3%), system crashes (8.5%), spacing and punctuation (7%), library location codes (6.3%), and Dewey decimal system (2.8%)."[2] Online catalogs, along with such accepted library practices as using Dewey Decimal Classification, Library of Congress subject headings, and rule-based bibliographic records, can be considered barriers to successful information retrieval by young children.

Solutions to the problems that children have with online catalogs range from improved interface design to revised cataloging practices. Research suggests several ways to improve interface design. Screens could be made more readable for children. Information could be less dense, with fewer screens to read. Spellcheckers could be added to help children overcome spelling difficulties. Using a mouse to click on options would eliminate the need to type. Browse displays can provide children with the opportunity to recognize subjects, rather than having to think of correct terminology. Systems need to be less strict with regard to spacing and punctuation. Voice synthesis might be a possible alternative to typing queries. The problem of dealing with ambiguous queries might be resolved by offering strategy options. For example, if a search term is ambiguous, a system might respond with: a list of words the query is alphabetically adjacent to, a list of synonyms or related words, a spellchecker, a help screen, or a directive to try another search with a more "walk-through" approach. Users who experience an unsuccessful search may need specific help to identify the problem and correct it. A system that accommodates children at all stages would be preferable. Children gradually need to make the transition from a simple system to a more advanced system of retrieval.

Two current products have incorporated many of the concepts necessary for successful children's retrieval. The Science Library Catalog was developed at the University of California at Los Angeles (UCLA) Graduate School of Library and Information Science. This is a browsing interface that provides access to science materials for children. It utilizes a Dewey decimal hierarchical approach based on children's recognition knowledge. The interface consists of a bookshelf screen that shows categories and subcategories of topics. Children can move through the bookshelves using a mouse to point and click on topics. Children are then presented with a book list. The lowest level of screens is the book record display screen, which provides bibliographic information and a library map for children to click on to find the location of a book. Children can use this interface with no prior training. It is not necessary to type, spell, or think of words with which to search.

Kid's Catalog, designed by Carl Corporation, is a catalog interface that can be used by children at all levels of cognitive development. Through use of several modes, children can progress from a recognition mode called "Explore" to a "Type Search" recall mode for more advanced users. The "Explore" mode utilizes colorful icons that represent categories of books most requested by children. Children can point and click on these icons to find subjects desired. These categories are presented in a visual hierarchy and one icon will retrieve titles that cover many related aspects of a subject. For example, a search on a particular country provides information on geography, history, art, cooking, and folklore for that country. The "Find It" mode provides lists of authors, titles, series, and subjects in alphabetical order for children to choose from, thus alleviating the need to type. The "Best Stories" mode links kids to popular materials that are chosen by staff. Whenever a child finds a title, he or she can click on a map of the library that flashes the location of the book. Although children still need some instruction to take full advantage of the interface, they are experiencing more success with *Kid's Catalog* than with standard online catalogs.

Kid's Catalog is an excellent example of an interface that is based on children's cognitive skills. It incorporates natural language in its categories, and it can be customized as children's information needs change.

Improved cataloging practices can also enhance children's access to materials. Catalogers must be aware of using language that children can read and understand when assigning subject headings, writing summaries, and establishing headings. Subject headings such as the Library of Congress Children's Headings assigned by the Annotated Card Program are appropriate for children. The "Guidelines for Standardized Cataloging of Children's Materials" suggest assigning both broad and specific subject headings and assigning both popular and scientific terms. Implementing these ideas will help children achieve more successful searches.

A cataloger must be attentive to a book's "aboutness." Applying headings consistently enhances retrieval. It is important to bring out topics in fiction as well as nonfiction materials. Sometimes more abstract headings, such as **Fear of the dark—Fiction**, are warranted. Catalogers should try to use summary notes for relevant keyword access by including natural language terms.

Children's materials come in a variety of formats. A juvenile collection can contain the same title in the form of a book, a sound recording, a videorecording, a large-print book, a book/cassette set, and a filmstrip, to name a few. Applying the same subject headings and summaries for the same work in different formats will increase the consistency of retrieval of these items. Other important access points include uniform titles and series statements. Uniform titles should be used for stories with many versions (AACR2 25.12B). Also, uniform titles provide important links to motion pictures and television programs. Many items published for children seem to be part of a series. Children often ask for these items, so providing access to series information is important.

When cataloging an item that is a collection of materials, it is necessary to provide access to the individual titles included in the collection. Titles listed in a contents note may, in some systems, be accessed using a keyword mode. Because children prefer the browse mode of searching, titles should also be traced for browse access whenever possible. Tracing alternative forms of titles also improves access. Titles that include punctuation (such as apostrophes), acronyms, or hyphenated words should be traced in alternative forms to help children find them.

These suggestions depend on how an automated system is designed. It is essential to understand how the system installed in your library is indexed. For example, in one system, the summary note may be indexed for keyword access in a subject context. Names of scientists in a collective biography may be included in the summary note, rather than in the contents note, thus providing relevant subject access. Punctuation can also affect searching. Even Boolean searching is not the same for all systems. It is critical to find out how a system treats searches. Catalogers can enhance access when they understand their users and how their system works.

Online catalogs have shown improvement over the years, but the search functions have not changed much. Online catalogs are still based on catalog cards. To satisfy today's information needs, catalogs must be based on searching behavior. Librarians know from working at a reference desk that patrons seeking information cannot always ask the question clearly or with great precision. Many times, they need some information in order to proceed or to verbalize a question. Online catalogs do not accommodate this natural way of seeking information. Online catalogs require users to know what they want before they begin a search. "We need cataloging to become a more dynamic process, a process that adds connections to materials and ideas as relationships become apparent."[3] Through use of such technology as Hypertext, users may eventually be able to answer information questions.

Online catalogs are an integral part of a library's total information system. They represent the starting point for information searching. As local area networks are being set up and connected to distant databases, providing smooth transitions between various interfaces becomes even more critical. It all begins with good cataloging.

Will we need to change the way we catalog items? Will MARC records cease to be the standard? Any system of the future must accommodate MARC records, because that has been our basis for cataloging and retrieval for some time. However, the catalogs of the future may expand upon current technology and cataloging practices to accommodate our understanding of searching behavior.

We must teach young people to navigate "the information superhighway" effectively. A combined effort from schools, parents, and public libraries is needed. Computers are becoming easier to use, but information will remain complex. Computer literacy in the future will mean more than just the ability to operate a computer; it will embrace the notion of retrieving information successfully. Whatever the future holds, we must keep children in mind and continue to meet their evolving information needs.

Notes

1. Virginia A. Walter, Christine L. Borgman, and Sandra G. Hirsh, "The Science Library Catalog: A Springboard for Information Literacy," *School Library Media Quarterly* 24 (Winter 1996): 109.
2. Pam Sandlian, "Rethinking the Rules," *School Library Journal* 47 (July 1995): 24.
3. Ibid., 25.

Bibliography

Anglo-American Cataloguing Rules. 2d ed., 1988 rev. Edited by Michael Gorman and Paul W. Winkler. Chicago: American Library Association, 1988.

Borgman, Christine L. "Why Are Online Catalogs Still Hard to Use?" *Journal of the American Society for Information Science* 47, no. 7 (July 1996): 493-503.

Borgman, Christine L., Sandra G. Hirsh, and Virginia A. Walter. "Children's Searching Behavior on Browsing and Keyword Online Catalogs: The Science Library Catalog Project." *Journal of the American Society for Information Science* 46, no. 9 (October 1995): 663-684.

Busey, Paula, and Tom Doerr. "Kid's Catalog: An Information Retrieval System for Children." *Journal of Youth Services in Libraries* 7, no. 1 (Fall 1993): 77-84.

DeHart, Florence E., and Marylouise D. Meder. "Cataloging Children's Materials: A Stage of Transition." In *Cataloging Special Materials: Critiques and Innovations,* edited by Sanford Berman. Phoenix, Ariz.: Oryx Press, 1986.

Drabenstott, Karen M., and Marjorie S. Weller. "Handling Spelling Errors in Online Catalog Searches." *Library Resources & Technical Services* 40, no. 2 (April 1996): 113-132.

Edmonds, Leslie, Paula Moore, and Kathleen Mehaffey Balcom. "The Effectiveness of an Online Catalog." *School Library Journal* 36 (October 1990): 28-32.

Gruber, Howard E., and J. Jacques Voneche, eds. *The Essential Piaget.* New York: Basic Books, 1977.

"Guidelines for Standardized Cataloging of Children's Materials." In *Cataloging for Kids: An Introduction to the Tools,* edited by Sharon Zuidervcld. Resources and Technical Services Division/CCS Cataloging of Children's Materials Committee. Chicago: American Library Association, 1991.

Hooten, Patricia A. "Online Catalogs: Will They Improve Children's Access?" *Journal of Youth Services in Libraries* 2, no. 3 (Spring 1989): 267–272.

Jacobson, Frances F. "From Dewey to Mosaic: Considerations in Interface Design for Children." *Internet Research* 5, no. 2 (1995): 67–73.

Martinez, Michael E. "Access to Information Technologies among School-Age Children: Implications for a Democratic Society." *Journal of the American Society for Information Science* 45, no. 6 (July 1994): 395–400.

Moore, Penelope A., and Alison St. George. "Children as Information Seekers: The Cognitive Demands of Books and Library Systems." *School Library Media Quarterly* 19 (Spring 1991): 161–168.

Sandlian, Pam. "Kid's Catalog: The Global Village Deciphered." *Colorado Libraries* 20 (Spring 1994): 23–25.

———. "Rethinking the Rules." *School Library Journal* 47 (July 1995): 22–25.

Solomon, Paul. "Information Systems for Children: Explorations in Information Access and Interface Usability for an Online Catalog in an Elementary School Library." Ph.D. diss., University of Maryland, 1991.

Thomsen, Elizabeth B. (March 17, 1995). CL-CAT and Kids: Observations about Children's Searching Skills. Libsplus Discussion Group. [Online] Available e-mail: libsplus@reading.ac.uk

Walter, Virginia A., Christine L. Borgman, and Sandra G. Hirsh. "The Science Library Catalog: A Springboard for Information Literacy." *School Library Media Quarterly* 24 (Winter 1996): 105–110.

8

Dewey Considerations

Frances E. Corcoran

T HE PURPOSE OF CLASSIFICATION is to arrange a collection, not to place a single item. Users who browse expect to find like subjects together. An efficient arrangement depends on familiarity with a collection, its contents, the reasons for its existence, and the purpose of its users.[1]

The Dewey Decimal Classification (DDC), as it is commonly modified in libraries for children, blends the two objectives outlined above by Miller and Terwillegar. It brings like subjects together, yet allows for broad groupings that reflect the reasons for the library's existence and the purpose of its users. The Dewey decimal schedules cover all subjects, but fiction is often placed in a separate alphabetic file without Dewey notation.

The basic Dewey subject arrangement is so familiar that it hardly needs introduction. There are 10 main classes, each divided into 10 divisions, each, in turn, subdivided into 10 sections. All numbers must be at least three digits long. When a need arises for further specificity, a decimal point is used, and the numbers are subdivided decimally as far as is necessary. Representative main classes are 200 for religion and 300 for social sciences. Sample social science divisions are 330 for economics and 370 for education. Typical sections in education are 372 for elementary education and 374 for adult education. Elementary education can be further subdivided—for example, 372.6 to indicate language arts. Thus, narrow subjects are arranged in a simple hierarchy under broad subjects in a way most users (including children) find easy to learn.

The use of Dewey is advocated for all media, both print and nonprint. In this way nonfiction media are grouped by subject and, if shelved together, are available for browsers wanting a variety of materials for their use. Using the top shelf of a book stack for audiovisual items keeps such items in proximity to the corresponding print editions. However, whether nonprint media are shelved together with print, nearby, or in a completely different area, what is important to the browsing patron is the classification consistency.

Dewey currently prefers putting biographical materials in the subject area of the biographee instead of a separate category in the 920s or a collection entitled Biography without Dewey classification. The subject number with the standard subdivision 092 added reflects this preference as does the Cataloging-in-Publication (CIP) data found on the title page verso. Once a decision is made on how to handle biographies, the person in charge of technical services should make a note of the preference and take care that biographical materials are classified consistently. Because some teachers require biographical reading, many school libraries house their biographical collection together for easier student use.

The Dewey staff is interested in the opinions of grassroots catalogers and will take into consideration their comments and suggestions. The staff researches possible changes before putting them into effect. The publication *DC&* offers changes made between editions. Occasionally a separate publication is issued to get the major changes into catalogers' hands as soon as possible. This happened in 1985 when the new computer science schedule 004–006 was produced to meet the needs of catalogers classifying software. The resulting classification offers a provision for arrangement by programming language, by computer model, or by specific program. Special purpose software is classed with the appropriate subject.

Two editions of the *Dewey Decimal Classification and Relative Index* are available: the abridged, which shortens the numbers, and the four-volume unabridged version.[2] Use of the unabridged edition allows greater specificity in the classification of a title because it provides longer numbers. This detail is appreciated in an academic or large public library, but children find a multitude of numbers confusing. A local policy may be adopted limiting the length of the number of decimal places to ease the location and reshelving of materials by students. The prime marks in the Dewey numbers in CIP or other LC cataloging records indicate logical places where long numbers may be cut. They mark either the end of the number from the abridged edition or the beginning of a standard subdivision from the DDC tables. Both current editions incorporate a manual on the use of the classification, which is an indispensable tool for the correct interpretation of the schedules.

A good example of response to suggestions from users is a revision in Folklore that appeared in the April 1994 issue of *DC&*. Folklore is usually a large part of the nonfiction section in a children's collection. The revision consisted of making provisions for specific kinds of folktales under the development of folklore of specific areas in 398.209. After adding the country number (for example, 398.209__43__ for Germany), one adds notation for kind of tale (for example, 398.2094305 for German ghost story). The result is to group works by country, reflecting a prevailing method of studying the literature of a country while also studying its geography and history. The revision has been incorporated in edition 21 published in 1996. In the abridged edition 13, notation for kind of folktale is not added; German ghost stories are simply classed in 398.20943. Catalogers may use the abridged version for this collection while using the unabridged for the collection as a whole. Other methods, such as using the country name under the 398.209 class number, are practiced but are not sanctioned by Dewey.

The twenty-first edition of the DDC includes several important changes that reflect user input over time. The three major revisions are: public administration (351–354), which is a complete revision; education (370), which is an extensive but relatively light revision; and the life sciences (560–590), which is a mix of complete and extensive revisions.

The most visible revision in education is to relocate the education of women from 376 and religious schools from 377 to subdivisions of 371 where education of women joins education of other kinds of students, and religious schools has a place with other kinds of schools. Home schools are moved from 649 to 371. Elementary reading (372.4) and language arts (372.6) have been greatly expanded.

The 570s (biology in general) have been completely revised. The most important feature is that the span on internal biological systems (571–575) includes the physiology of specific kinds of plants and animals formerly in 580–590. The most notable change in the rest of the life sciences is a revision of 597 and 599 to give greater specificity with short numbers for popular fishes and mammals. In making changes, a conscious effort was made to avoid unnecessary reuse of numbers. For example, 574, the number in which most works on general biology were formerly classed, has been left vacant.

A second classification help, if your library uses it, is *Sears List of Subject Headings,* an H. W. Wilson publication.[3] This book includes suggested numbers from the abridged edition of DDC. The Dewey numbers given in Sears are intended to suggest where to begin your search but must be reviewed to be sure they are consistent with your library practice. Catalogers using Sears should mark their Sears copy with the Dewey number selected for that subject so that subsequent inquiries will note that choice.

Some audiovisual producers suggest classification numbers in their documentation or on cataloging included with purchases. These should also be verified against the existing collection before they are integrated into the main catalog. The goal is consistency for the sake of the browsing patron.

Because only one classification number may be used for an item covering a variety of subjects, the deciding factor in selecting a number is your patrons' main focus—that is, the curriculum for a school or community interest for a public library. Subject headings will provide access to additional aspects of the work. The purpose of classification is to arrange a collection efficiently, which will, in turn, make the collection user friendly.

Many children's collections are divided into broad groups so that beginning readers can easily find material they can read and understand. Materials in the early reader section may have a prefix in the call number, for example, "E" for easy books or "P" for primary or picture books. One of the first reading readiness skills involves the ability to categorize objects, and Dewey enhances this skill if it is used for all nonfiction, including easy books. Classification of materials also helps teach children the difference between fiction and nonfiction. Consistency is evident again in the use of the first three letters (the number of letters is a local option) of the author's last name or the title, if no author is credited, in both fiction and nonfiction call numbers.

Notes

1. Rosalind E. Miller and Jane C. Terwillegar, *Commonsense Cataloging: A Cataloger's Manual,* 4th ed., rev. (New York: H. W. Wilson, 1990), 87.

2. Melvil Dewey, *Abridged Dewey Decimal Classification and Relative Index,* ed. Joan S. Mitchell, Julianne Beall, Winton E. Matthews Jr., and Gregory R. New, 13th ed. (Albany, N.Y.: OCLC Forest Press, 1997); and Melvil Dewey, *Dewey Decimal Classification and Relative Index,* ed. Joan S. Mitchell, Julianne Beall, Winton E. Matthews Jr., and Gregory R. New, 21st ed. (Albany, N.Y.: OCLC Forest Press, 1996).

3. *Sears List of Subject Headings,* ed. Joseph Miller, 16th ed. (New York: H. W. Wilson, 1997).

9

Sources for Dewey Numbers

Gregory R. New

SINCE 1980, THE BIGGEST single source for Dewey Decimal Classification numbers for American libraries has been the Library of Congress. In the early days, the source was called "DC on LC," that is, Dewey Classification numbers on Library of Congress cards. For 35 years, Dewey numbers were added to records for 20,000 to 30,000 titles per year. From 1966 to 1975, there was a spurt of growth, and each year since then, LC has supplied Dewey numbers for over 100,000 titles per year.

These numbers appear in the MARC tapes sold by the LC Cataloging Distribution Service (CDS). The tapes are the original source of cataloging information that many libraries obtain when they buy cards from vendors or download electronic records from bibliographic utilities.

Other libraries also contribute Dewey numbers to bibliographic utilities, however. Thus, one may not always be able to tell who did the original classification that helps readers find their way in book collections. But probably a great majority of the Dewey numbers in most American libraries were originally assigned at the Library of Congress. Many classifiers in other institutions who contribute Dewey numbers lean upon LC work even when they must do their own.

The Dewey Family

Several large and important institutions cooperate to maintain the Dewey Decimal Classification. They may be thought of as the Dewey family. It is an extended family; the major branches include parts of the Library of Congress, OCLC, and the American Library Association.

Most of the staff work is done in the Decimal Classification Division at the Library of Congress. The application of the Classification, currently running about 110,000 titles per year, is supported by appropriated funds like most work of federal agencies. The editing, however, is done under a contract with Forest Press (a division of OCLC), which holds the Dewey copyright. Forest Press obtains the funds that support the editing largely from the sale of full and abridged editions of the Classification and related products such as Dewey for Windows and *Subject Headings for Children: A List of Subject Headings Used by the Library of Congress with Dewey Numbers Added.*

Forest Press actually goes back much further than OCLC. In fact, it goes back to 1911, when Melvil Dewey gave edition 7 of his Classification the Forest Press imprint. The Press later became the de facto heir to the DDC copyrights that Melvil Dewey assigned to the Lake Placid Club Education Foundation in 1922. The decision to move the DDC editorial offices to LC came in 1923. By contrast, the purchase of Forest Press by OCLC in 1988 is recent history.

The link between Forest Press and LC provides an ideal editorial environment for successive editions of the Classification. Since 1930, that environment has included a link with Dewey Classification practice. The link with OCLC is proving to be equally beneficial by enabling the Classification to become an integral part of an increasingly sophisticated electronic world. For example, OCLC Research played a major role in developing Dewey for Windows, a Microsoft Windows–based version of edition 21 on a compact disc.

The American Library Association officially came into the picture in 1953 when a DC Committee was reconstituted as the DC Editorial Policy Committee (EPC). Of its ten members, four represent ALA. An additional four members are selected by Forest Press: its executive director and three others. Currently, one of the Forest Press appointees represents the National Library of Canada and another represents the Australian Committee on Cataloguing. The ninth member represents the (British) Library Association, and the tenth is the Associate Librarian of Congress for Library Services.

The representatives on EPC are not the only link with ALA. Whenever a large or difficult revision is on the drawing boards, EPC approaches the ALCTS CCS Subject Analysis Committee (SAC) to appoint a review subcommittee for that schedule. For example, SAC subcommittees reviewed the revised versions of education, public administration, and biology schedules for the current edition. Also, EPC asks for and obtains subcommittees to review the numbers and manual notes that appear in each abridged edition.

Editors check with the Cataloging of Children's Materials Committee and the Cataloging Needs of Public Libraries Committee for matters affecting their respective constituencies. These committees reviewed and endorsed the recent revisions in folklore and holidays. They also suggested members for the SAC subcommittees to review the abridged edition and the education revision. DC editors approach both committees from time to time for advice about what kinds of material and what languages should be given priority in classification.

Editors also approach other groups on matters on which they have expertise, for example, the ALA Committee on Cataloging: Asian and African Materials, and the Special Libraries Association.

The three members of the Editorial Policy Committee from the United Kingdom, Canada, and Australia are symbolic of the international reach of the Dewey family. The United Kingdom member has always been chair of the (British) Library Association's Dewey Decimal Classification Committee. That Committee plays a role similar to that of a standing SAC review subcommittee.

All members of the Dewey family mentioned so far contribute to the English editions. There are also various ad hoc groups that must be organized to translate Dewey. For each of the several current translations, three principal groups must be brought together. First, there must be a funding source that can be confident that its investment will bear fruit. Second, there must be a mechanism to obtain a consensus within a nation or (sometimes) a large family of nations on the degree to which Dewey must be adapted to the needs of a given language and culture. Finally, there must be a team of qualified translators.

Editing the Classification

There is one editor, Joan Mitchell, and three assistant editors. Ms. Mitchell came to the Division in 1993 from Carnegie Mellon

University, where she was director of education technology. She had served on the Editorial Policy Committee since 1985, and was its chair for a year. She is also well known in ALA, where she was chair or member of a variety of committees, notably, chair of the Subject Analysis Committee and of the Cataloging and Classification Section.

The three assistant editors have all had long experience as classifiers. Winton Matthews and I joined the Decimal Classification Division in 1968, and became assistant editors in 1985. Julianne Beall joined the Division in 1977, and became assistant editor in 1986. Each editor confers with classifiers on problem books and classifies, as time permits, in the area she or he edits. Editors also field classification questions from outside the Division, thus remaining connected to the world that the Classification serves.

Not long after an edition is published, each editor begins preparing drafts of the schedules in his or her area for the next edition. In preparation for editions 20 and 21, about nine-tenths of the schedules were divided among the assistant editors. The editor got the balance, in addition to bearing the overall responsibility.

As each draft is prepared, it is carefully reviewed by the other editors. Usually there is a second round of drafts and reviews. Final drafts are prepared as "exhibits" for the Editorial Policy Committee. EPC normally meets twice a year for a two- or three-day session. Schedules with relatively minor revisions are usually approved subject to various suggestions. The approval consists of a recommendation to Forest Press that the revised schedule be published in the forthcoming edition.

When a drastic revision occurs, EPC will usually recommend that the schedule be sent out for review. This is when SAC is called upon to appoint a review subcommittee. Other committees, associations, and individual experts are also approached. Normally the review process takes about two years. The more favorable the reviews, the greater the chance that the revision will be approved when the EPC next considers it.

Sometimes the reviews are not favorable, and the proposed revision must go back for more work, often being recast in the process. The three most significant revisions in the current edition 21 all went through two or more rounds of reviews. Most notable of these is the life sciences revision, on which I began working in 1972, four years after joining the Division. When doing a major revision, staff members subscribe to the formula that the Supreme Court made famous: "Proceed with all deliberate speed."

Classifying Library Material

The Division currently has eight full-time classifiers, who classify about 10,000 titles each per year. At one time there were twelve full-time classifiers, but the Classification Division has had to find ways to do more with less, just as most other librarians have. In addition to the full-timers, both the chief of the Division and the team leader do substantial classifying. Finally, there are two or three persons in other LC cataloging divisions who have been trained to classify in art, education, and recreation.

The eight full-time people are called Decimal Classification Specialists. They are assigned broad, overlapping subject specialties. For example, two share responsibility for science and technology (500 and 600). One concentrates on languages and literature (400 and 800), another on history (900), while a third covers both of these areas as needed. In addition, each classifier has backup specialties so that all fields are covered regardless of the number of absentees. The chief and team leader also have their subject specialties.

The classifiers work very much as a team. The work atmosphere is relaxed, and classifiers freely consult with each other and the editors on classification problems and pitch in to maintain an even work flow. The classifiers are also ready, as time permits, to entertain questions from users on application and interpretation of the Classification.

In one way, the work situation in the Division differs from that of almost everyone else in the library profession: there are no backlogs. Staff members assign Dewey numbers to about two-thirds of the full cataloging records distributed by LC, but over a quarter of the material never even comes to this office. For example, the Cyrillic alphabet material bypasses the Division. But even when the material does come here, the Division operates on a five-day turnaround. That is, staff must send on anything that cannot be classified within a week of receiving it. When the work flow is light, Division members cover all material for which Dewey numbers will be useful. When the work flow is heavy, however, some material must be sent on without Dewey numbers.

It is a situation that requires a good sense of priorities. CIPs (the Cataloging-in-Publication records) are always covered, usually on a one-day turnaround. In addition, most American and British trade publications are covered, as are works of reference value in the major Western European languages. Sometimes government publications and pamphlets are sent on, but as many as possible of these are done. Good judgment of the staff serves as a kind of regulator. Although children's libraries are not an explicit focus, the Division generally covers the books that they most need to have classified, and confine the gaps mostly to material that they least need.

Comparable Dewey numbers are available from other national sources of centralized cataloging copy, such as the British Library in *British National Bibliography* and the National Library of Canada in *Canadiana, Canada's National Bibliography*. When the centralized cataloging is part of a CIP program, the numbers appear in the publications themselves, usually on the back of the title page.

In addition, member libraries of union catalogs maintained by bibliographic utilities such as OCLC and RLIN (Research Library Information Network) often contribute cataloging copy that includes a Dewey number. Vendors that supply cards or cataloging copy to individual libraries usually copy from existing sources, but do original cataloging when necessary.

When a library is considering a Dewey number found in a bibliographic utility, the MARC coding of the classification number field is a useful aid in evaluating the number. Standard practice is for the number to be in the 082 field. A subfield code called the second indicator (source of call number) must be checked to determine whether the number is supplied by LC or another library. If supplied by LC, the second indicator is set to 0; if supplied by an outside library, the second indicator is set to 4.

Although an outside library number is often a good one, it may reflect practices and options that differ widely from those adopted by LC classifiers. Also, classifiers in some outside libraries may not be as well trained as classifiers at LC. Thus, numbers with a second indicator 4 should be checked. Normally numbers assigned by LC can be accepted, provided that they conform to the accepting library's own practices and options. For example, a children's collection classed by the abridged edition will need only one or two segments of a three-segment number.

OCLC has established a special field, 092 (locally assigned Dewey call number), for Dewey numbers supplied by its member libraries. The 082 field is used in the OCLC Online Union Catalog (OLUC) by national agencies that generally conform to LC practice, but other member libraries may use either the 092 field, or the 082 field with second indicator set to 4.

Recently the Library of Congress has begun to utilize copy cataloging, which involves starting with an outside library's Dewey number if one appears in the 082 field with valid information in subfield 2 showing which edition the number came from. If the number is verified or corrected by the Decimal Classification Division or one of the classifiers trained by the Division, the second indicator is set to 0, the same as if the number were originally assigned by LC. Otherwise, the copied number remains set to 4. Once LC has adapted the records, they are distributed on MARC tapes as Library of Congress records. Only the second indicator tells whether the Dewey number has been verified (value 0) or simply been copied without review (value 4).

In summary, an impressive supply of Dewey numbers is already available for works added to children's collections. About 110,000 a year come from the Library of Congress, but utilities like OCLC and RLIN, vendors, and other libraries also make substantial contributions.

Future Possibilities

Two initiatives at OCLC promise to enhance the availability and convenience of Dewey numbers. The first is represented by OCLC's NetFirst database, which includes DDC numbers assigned to over 40,000 records of Internet-accessible resources. Other noncommercial World Wide Web sites are also utilizing the hierarchical structure of Dewey to provide subject approaches to Web-accessible documents. For example, "CyberDewey: A Guide to Internet Resources Organized Using Dewey Decimal Classification Codes" is available at: http://ivory.lm.com/~mundie/DDHC/DDH.html. Such sources are now in their infancy. They can be expected to develop quickly over the next few years.

The second initiative is an exploration of the feasibility of adding Cutter-table book numbers to DDC class numbers in the OCLC OLUC. Initial plans call for using both the Cutter-Sanborn and Cutter three-figure tables. Author symbols are now perhaps the least standardized area of cataloging. But if a single, current source containing millions of bibliographic records becomes available for Cutter numbers that can be added to Dewey numbers, even author symbols may respond to standardization.

10

Sears List of
Subject Headings

Joseph Miller

TWO PRINCIPAL SOURCES of subject headings exist for cataloging children's materials. The first is *Library of Congress Subject Headings* (LCSH) together with the modified list of Annotated Card (AC) Program headings used by the Library of Congress for children's materials only. The AC headings are found in the front of the first volume of the print edition of LCSH and also in electronic form. The second source is *Sears List of Subject Headings* (Sears). These two lists are both subject authority environments entirely complete within themselves, and a library will use either one or the other, but never both.

The need for two authority lists was felt early in the twentieth century. In 1923, when the Sears List first appeared, the Library of Congress *Subject Headings Used in the Dictionary Catalogs of the Library of Congress* and the American Library Association's *List of Subject Headings for Use in Dictionary Catalogs* already existed. Then as now, the Library of Congress tailored its subject headings to its own needs, which are those of a very large research library and quite different from the cataloging needs of small libraries. It was with this difference in mind that Minnie Earl Sears consulted the catalogs of a number of small libraries that she considered well cataloged and put together a list entitled *List of Subject Headings for Small Libraries*. Beginning with the sixth edition (1950), the work was given her name and has since been known as the Sears

List. The Sears List has never been intended exclusively for cataloging children's materials. It is meant to be used in any kind of small library.

The original plan of the Sears List was to remain as close as possible to the usage of the Library of Congress in order to make it possible for a library to change over from Sears headings to LC headings when it grew larger. Since that time, however, the two worlds of Sears and LCSH have grown more distinct and separate, although they still share important common ground. Both are alphabetical subject lists, not true thesauri. Both are based on the principle of precoordinated subject strings with the use of subdivisions rather than discrete terms to be coordinated by the end user. Both are based upon literary warrant and make no attempt to establish headings before there are materials requiring such headings. And both are devised for the implementation of Cutter's Rule for the cataloging of materials to the greatest possible level of specificity.

Although Sears continues to maintain conformity to the usage of the Library of Congress insofar as it is possible, nonetheless a number of differences exist between the two lists. In general, Sears has fewer technical terms, preferring the common names of things over the scientific names. Sears allows for direct geographic subdivisions rather than indirect. For example, Sears would have **Bridges— Chicago (Ill.)** where LC would have **Bridges—Illinois—Chicago**. Beginning with the fifteenth edition Sears converted all its remaining inverted headings to the uninverted form while LC maintains a combination of inverted and uninverted headings. Now, for example, **Education, Elementary** in LC will be **Elementary education** in Sears. These differences must be kept in mind when LC MARC records or LC Cataloging-in-Publication (CIP) data are being adapted for a catalog using Sears headings. The greatest difference between the two lists is that, apart from the application of standard subdivisions, the Library of Congress establishes in its list every heading it has used in its catalog. Sears, on the other hand, is not attached to any one catalog and aims instead to be a pattern or model for the creation of headings as needed. As a result it is less detailed and complete than LCSH but also much smaller and more flexible. In Sears, for example, at the heading **Animals** there is a general reference note authorizing the creation of headings for kinds of animals and species of animals as needed. Likewise, at **Dogs**, there is a provision for creating headings for breeds of dogs as needed. The cataloger is not encouraged to put a book on Collies under **Dogs**, but in very small libraries that is always an option. Even when there is no general reference note in Sears providing for kinds of things and names of specific things under the heading for the thing, it is implied by the nature of the system that those headings can always be created. In the front of the Sears List is a list of commonly used subdivisions, but again this is not meant to be all-inclusive nor to restrict catalogers from using other subdivisions where they are needed.

Both LCSH and Sears are now printed in a thesaurus-like display with broader, narrower, and related terms in the list indicated with the labels BT, NT, and RT. This change from the more obscure *X, XX, See,* and *See also* makes the Sears volume easier for catalogers to use. It can be helpful to end users at the catalog as well, both in refining their search terms and as a rough-and-ready index to the stacks by way of the Dewey Decimal Classification (DDC) numbers given in Sears. The DDC numbers in Sears are meant only as pointers to the place or places in the Classification where materials on a particular subject are most likely to be found, not as a guide for classifying or finding any individual book. Furthermore, when the editions of Sears and the DDC do not coincide, the numbers in Sears can be out of date in certain parts of the Classification.

One obvious advantage of the Sears List over LCSH for a small library is its size. The entire list is contained in one handy volume, while LCSH is now four very large volumes with cross-references spanning the set. The Sears List is correspondingly cheaper. The fifteenth edition sells for $49, while the nineteenth edition of LCSH is $200. (Prices are given in U.S. dollars.)

One disadvantage of Sears is that a new edition is published only every three years, while a new edition of LCSH appears every year. Sears produces an updated magnetic tape version annually, but it is available only to users with mainframe computers, mostly vendors. When a need for new headings arises between editions of Sears, catalogers can always take those headings from CIP, LC MARC records, periodical indexes, or from other sources and incorporate them into the structure of the Sears List, that is, by linking them to the appropriate broader term and establishing cross-references to any narrower or related terms already in the List.

In the era of MARC records and cooperative cataloging there is sometimes pressure on libraries to switch from Sears headings to LC headings. This is a decision that every library must make for itself, based on the perceived advantages and disadvantages of the two subject heading systems. Ideally, that decision is made by a librarian with the interests of the users in mind rather than by an administrator who knows nothing about cataloging. It is not necessary to abandon Sears headings in order to use MARC records. There is full provision in the USMARC bibliographic format for using Sears headings in the 650 field, with the value 7 in the second indicator position and the code *sears* in subfield 2. In the OCLC MARC format, Sears headings are identified by the value 8 in the second indicator position without a subfield 2. Most vendors are able to supply MARC records with Sears headings.

The "Principles of the Sears List of Subject Headings," which can be found in the front of every edition, serves as a substantial introduction both to the Sears List and to the practice of subject cataloging in general. The same principles of subject analysis are applicable to Sears as to other subject heading lists, but the shortness and simplicity of the Sears List make it especially practical for small libraries, especially libraries devoted primarily to children's materials.

Bibliography

Chan, Lois Mai, Phyllis A. Richmond, and Elaine Svenonius, eds. *Theory of Subject Analysis: A Sourcebook*. 2d ed. Littleton, Colo.: Libraries Unlimited, 1990.

Cutter, Charles. *Rules for a Dictionary Catalog*. 4th ed. Washington, D.C.: U.S. Government Printing Office, 1904.

Ferl, Terry Ellen, and Larry Millsap. *Subject Cataloging: A How-to-Do-It Workbook*. New York: Neal-Schuman, 1991.

Foskett, A. C. *The Subject Approach to Information*. 5th ed. London: The Library Association, 1996.

Miller, Rosalind E., and Jane C. Terwillegar. *Commonsense Cataloging: A Cataloger's Manual*. 4th ed., rev. New York: H. W. Wilson, 1990.

Sears List of Subject Headings. 15th ed. Edited by Joseph Miller. New York: H. W. Wilson, 1994.

Sears List of Subject Headings: Canadian Companion. 5th ed. Edited by Lynne Lighthall. New York: H. W. Wilson, 1995.

Wynar, Bohdan S. *Introduction to Cataloging and Classification*. 8th ed. Edited by Arlene G. Taylor. Littleton, Colo.: Libraries Unlimited, 1992.

11

Cataloging
Nonbook Materials

Jean Weihs

INFORMATION AND ENTERTAINMENT come in many different
formats, and children's libraries frequently have more diverse
media in their collections than do other types of libraries. Both
book and nonbook material in a collection should be cataloged so
that there is equal and adequate access to all sources of information
and entertainment. Children cannot be expected to know that the
uncataloged computer discs stored in the workroom will answer
their needs, and the librarian may not recall the specific subject
content of these discs even if she or he remembers their existence.
Not only is the time spent cataloging nonbook materials more than
regained in the speed of reference retrieval, but the effort is also re-
paid in the additional material being made available to the children.

A children's library should have only one catalog with the
whole collection listed there. A child may not know or remember
that different formats are found in different catalogs. Even if a child
does have this knowledge, multiple catalogs may convey the idea
that finding information and entertainment in a library setting is
tedious or difficult. A negative experience with the library's catalog
may color a child's perception of the library and, perhaps, extend
to related matters, such as reading and learning. It is important to
have an easy-to-use, integrated catalog.

Anglo-American Cataloguing Rules, second edition, 1988 revision (AACR2R), facilitates the construction of an integrated catalog

because it applies the same cataloging principles to all materials. These basic concepts are followed in rules designed for specific formats. In cataloging a particular type of material, the chapter in AACR2R devoted to that medium is consulted, together with the general rules chapter.

The type of material is indicated within the catalog record by a general material designation placed immediately after the title proper (the short title). The purpose of a general material designation is to give an early warning signal about the format of the item. For some media this designation also signals the need for equipment. General material designations are optional for all materials. However, in most American and Canadian children's libraries, general material designations are used for nonbook materials but not for books, pamphlets, and periodicals.

General material designations are always given in lowercase letters in the singular. The following is a list of general material designations for the nonbook materials most commonly found in children's libraries.

activity card	game	picture
art reproduction	globe	realia
chart	kit	slide
computer file	map	sound recording
diorama	microform	toy
filmstrip	model	transparency
flash card	motion picture	videorecording

An item may be described more precisely in the part of the record called "extent of item." For example, the extent of item may state "3 study prints" in a record with the general material designation "picture."

Most of the information given in the note area of the catalog record is optional. Information that is important to the effective use of the item being cataloged and that cannot be included in the more formal parts of the record should be given here, for example, necessary equipment. Summaries describe subject content objectively and succinctly. They are useful for items that cannot be scanned easily by children making selection decisions. However, summaries, which are time-consuming to write, are not necessary when the content of an item is adequately conveyed in the title or series statements.

In an integrated catalog the same list of subject headings is applied to all materials. The use of media form subdivisions, which are similar to the list of general material designations, will depend on a library's policies and the needs of the children it serves. Media form subdivisions divide a particular subject into format groupings. If a library wishes to emphasize that information and entertainment can come from many formats, media form subdivisions should not be used. On the other hand, media form subdivisions are advisable in libraries where children's subject requests are tied to format, for example, a videocassette about lions. Media form subdivisions are unnecessary and uneconomic in automated systems that can link subject headings and general material designations.

The use of the same classification scheme for books and nonbook materials will allow the whole collection to be intershelved in subject groupings, either in total intershelving where all items are housed in one classification sequence or in partial intershelving where the book collection is shelved together and the nonbook items in the same subject field are housed nearby. Classification can also be used to produce bibliographies in some automated systems. In addition, in an automated system, classification numbers can be used to help the librarian with the selection process by organizing holdings and usage data by subject area.

Technological developments produce new media that find their way onto library shelves before rules for cataloging these media can be codified and accepted internationally. In 1996, interactive multimedia and Internet resources had preliminary rules. *Guidelines for Bibliographic Description of Interactive Multimedia* and *Cataloging Internet Resources: A Manual and Practical Guide* are being used by libraries as interim standards. The use of these guidelines tests the rules for their effectiveness. After a period of gathering input, these documents may be revised and submitted to the international body that controls the *Anglo-American Cataloguing Rules.* Eventually rules for both interactive multimedia and Internet resources will be standardized. In the meantime, catalogers of children's materials should use these preliminary documents.

Fewer sources of catalog copy exist for nonbook materials than for books, and fewer commercial cataloging firms provide nonbook records. Therefore, the cataloging of nonbook materials for children's collections is more likely to be done locally. Instruction in, and ideas about, cataloging nonbook materials will be found in the sources listed in the Bibliography at the end of this work.

12

Filing in the Card Catalog

Pat Thomas

CONSIDER, IF YOU WILL, the purpose of a catalog. It is to provide access—by author, title, and subject—to everything that is cataloged in a library's collection. The catalog is an indispensable tool for all users of the library. If cards are not filed, they cannot provide that access. Conversely, if cards are misfiled, they are as good as lost and will never provide access to anything! Sobering thought, is it not?

If you are new to filing in a catalog, here are some things to keep in mind:

1. *How is the catalog arranged?* A dictionary catalog has all the entries (author, title, subject, series, etc.) and their related references arranged together in one alphabet, although their sub-arrangement frequently varies from the strictly alphabetical. No matter how you wish to search for an item, the advantage of this arrangement is that only one sequence of cards is consulted; many people prefer this "single look-up." A divided catalog, on the other hand, has more than one alphabetical sequence; cards are separated into subject and author/title sections. This arrangement is considered helpful in very large catalogs, where sheer bulk makes filing into and using the catalog difficult. However, it may cause the user to miss material because all entries are not interfiled together (for example, books written

by Charles Dickens and books *about* Charles Dickens as a subject are filed in separate catalogs).

2. *What rules are used to file in the catalog?* In order to be useful, a catalog must be consistent, and in order for it to be consistent, designated filing rules must be followed. The filer should be familiar with these rules and know how to use them when filing questions arise.

Two sets of filing rules are widely used: the American Library Association rules and the Library of Congress (LC) rules.[1] Both were revised in 1980 because computer sorting of entries required some modification of standard filing practices. Manual filing had always allowed some license in the filing of cards. For example, numerals that were not spelled out and abbreviations could be interfiled with entries in which the words were spelled in full. The computer is more literal and sorts the cards exactly as printed; numerals are filed before alphabetic character strings and abbreviations are filed as printed. Of course, these were not the only changes made when the filing rules were revised, but they serve as examples of the need to keep filing rules current with changes in technology. Many older catalogs were arranged according to earlier or local filing rules and probably should continue to be so filed. Whatever rules are used to file in your catalog, become very familiar with them for the sake of consistency.

After years of filing experience in several catalogs and after consulting a number of sources and editions of filing rules, one can observe common patterns or two basic rules:

1. Arrange all entries according to the order of the English alphabet.
2. Arrange word by word, alphabetizing letter by letter to the end of each word.

These sound simple enough, but questions inevitably arise as you file, and it is wise to refer to your copy of these rules often; don't depend on memory. Note in your rule book where an example for a specific rule can be found in the alphabetic catalog. Familiarity with filing rules will help you not only as a filer but also as a catalog user and as an instructor in the use of the catalog. Some say, in fact, that there is no better way to become familiar with a catalog, and with a collection as well, than by filing catalog cards. Filing offers an opportunity to become familiar with authors and titles and subject heading usage as well as with the arrangement of the catalog entries.

Self-Instruction Manual for Filing Catalog Cards is a helpful manual based on the ALA filing rules.[2] Using the 10 main rules, the manual leads the reader gently through the principles and practices of filing. Even if you use a different or earlier set of filing rules in your catalog, this manual is very useful because it explains the underlying problems so clearly. You can then modify its statements to answer your particular filing questions.

Filing in the catalog is seldom considered or discussed by staff in a media center or in the children's section of a public library. The press of more immediate concerns often relegates filing to a few extra moments whenever they are available or to whoever is willing to try her hand at this "thankless" task. Perhaps filing catalog cards deserves something better than that. Remember that a card misfiled represents an access point forever lost. Try to find some time to file when you will be uninterrupted. If you assign filing to a student assistant or to someone inexperienced, take the time to look over her or his work. (Have filers file above the rods and then drop the cards as they are checked.) Post the letters of the alphabet on or near the catalog; try a running strip on the front of the catalog near the top. You'll be surprised how your filing improves and how helpful it will be for the catalog users.

Notes

1. *ALA Filing Rules* (Chicago: American Library Association, 1980); and *Library of Congress Filing Rules,* prepared by John C. Rather and Susan C. Biebel (Washington, D.C.: Library of Congress, 1980).

2. Diane Foxhill Carothers, *Self-Instruction Manual for Filing Catalog Cards* (Chicago: American Library Association, 1981), o.p.

13

Automating the
Children's Catalog

Diane Stine

AUTOMATION OF LIBRARIES has changed the entire focus of
library service. In the past, record-keeping functions in the
library were so cumbersome that most of the librarian's time was
spent selecting, acquiring, and cataloging materials, checking these
items in and out, keeping up the inventory, securing overdues, and
maintaining the card catalog.

In the past 20 years, most libraries have introduced automation
for some or all of the preceding functions. As more and more
libraries have automated, the focus of the librarian has shifted from
record keeper to teacher, facilitator, reading consultant, and information provider. Even libraries that have not yet introduced automation have tried to move in this direction and have had to abandon
many of the clerical functions as these other roles are deemed
more important by administrators, teachers, and boards.

Most libraries began the automation process by introducing a
circulation system that checked books in and out, kept track of inventory, handled overdues, and provided reports of these functions.
The next level of sophistication added an online catalog that provided access to library items by author, title, subject, and often keyword and Boolean searching. The online catalog became a model for
teaching children searching skills and logic. Two stages in the development of online public access catalogs (OPACs) were described
by Michael Gorman early in the history of online catalogs.[1] Gorman

stated that in the "minimalist" stage the online records must contain at least as much information as catalog cards. After successful completion of a database of standard records comes the next stage—enhancement of records to improve access. OPAC systems improve access and expand on the content of the catalog record, and in the design of OPAC systems and cataloging enhancements, there has been some recognition that children have unique needs.

However, many libraries stopped the automation process with the circulation system. In these settings there was often a lack of understanding by administrators and boards. As far as they were concerned, they had already automated and did not understand the difference between a circulation system and an online catalog. In these buildings librarians either were forced to maintain a card catalog along with the circulation system or else abandoned the card catalog along with the access it provided. Schools that invested in circulation systems when this was the only option available overwhelmingly chose Follett's Circ+. Their circulation records consist of brief data needed for circulation purposes only: author, title, call number, and bar code.

A major issue in automating the children's catalog is conformity to the MAchine-Readable Cataloging (MARC) standard, discussed more fully in the chapter on MARC in this volume. MARC is a communications format, not a guarantee of cataloging content. The structure of a record must meet the MARC standard but the bibliographic data contained in the record may vary depending on the source of the cataloging. The Library of Congress (LC) distributes what might be called "pure" MARC records. The same records may be available from a bibliographic utility or on a CD-ROM database purchased from a vendor. Most of the OPAC systems currently on the market meet the MARC standard.

Some systems are described as MARC-compatible, which is defined by Walt Crawford as "the ability to process USMARC records directly . . . as needed, writing or restoring them, without loss of content, content designation, or structure."[2] Sometimes it is difficult to verify a vendor's claims, but a demonstration of the system should include, for example, the restoring of a MARC-compatible record to the MARC communications format, which contains the record directory needed in a minicomputer system.

At one time, the Microcomputer Library Interchange Format (MicroLIF) was considered substandard. (See the chapter on MicroLIF for a more complete discussion of this topic.) This format was initiated by some vendors to ensure the compatibility of automated processing and microcomputer OPAC software. However, the vendors who have joined forces in this consortium have made a commitment to adhere to the MARC standard. MicroLIF is another variation of MARC compatibility and is acceptable according to the guidelines described by Crawford.

Both the libraries with circulation systems and those with no automated systems need to have MARC or MARC-compatible records in order to implement an online catalog. When considering conversion options to obtain these records the librarian should keep the unique information needs of young library users in mind. Sears headings and Dewey call numbers may be considered more appropriate than LC for children's collections. Additional information such as reading level, interest level, and relation to curriculum may be required in the notes field.

There are several ways to obtain these MARC records:

1. Send a catalog card (preferably a shelflist card, if the library has maintained one) for each item in your library to a vendor who will match your title against its database and provide MARC records on discs or tapes as needed. Then your automation vendor will load those tapes or discs onto the system you choose for your catalog. The cost of this method varies from twenty-five cents to a dollar per record with bar code. Some vendors will create a record for non-hits (no match in the vendor's database) with information contained on your shelflist card. Other vendors will return non-hits for libraries to create their own records.

2. You can purchase software to create MARC records. You, your staff, or volunteers can enter data from your catalog card into a template and the program creates MARC records. Again, your online catalog provider will then load these records onto the system.

3. You can purchase a CD-ROM product with MARC records for many titles on it and you can search the CD to find records matching the titles in your collection. Then you can download these matching records onto discs or tapes or directly onto your online catalog if you have already purchased the system.

4. You can enter information title by title directly into your online catalog system.

5. You can use one of the cataloging programs like MICROCON from OCLC where you enter brief data onto discs. A vendor runs this brief data against its database looking for matches, which the vendor then provides on discs or tapes to be loaded onto your system.

6. Libraries that have brief automated records, such as on a Circ+ system, can give these records to a vendor on disks and have that vendor run the discs against its database and upgrade the records to MARC records to be loaded onto the online catalog system.

The more work the school library does itself, the less money it has to pay a vendor. However, you must also consider the time spent by library staff in choosing the best method for your library.

In addition to creating MARC records, each item must be bar-coded for circulation and inventory control purposes. Along with creating records and bar-coding comes choosing an automation system, including the program itself and the hardware needed to run it. It is important to speak with other librarians and to see the various programs demonstrated. Each library has its own needs and budget constraints that must be considered. Besides having the catalog available in the media center, many schools now have networked all computers in the school so that the catalog can be searched from the classroom and computer labs. The number of workstations to be accessing the catalog will be a factor in choosing your catalog and equipment.

As new items are purchased for your library you can usually buy MARC records for your items from the same vendor that supplies the materials. Most vendors now provide complete processing, including spine labels, catalog cards for a manual shelflist, MARC records, bar codes placed on the book, and book jackets. This entire package costs only about $1 per book and provides the library with shelf-ready materials. The only steps for the librarian are to load the MARC records onto the local system, place the books on the shelf, and file the shelflist card. Librarians are still debating whether it is necessary to maintain a manual shelflist as a backup. If you make backup tapes of your system regularly and keep these tapes off-site, a manual shelflist is probably not necessary.

Automating the library and purchasing shelf-ready materials frees the librarian from being a record keeper. Then she or he has the time to concentrate on providing reference service, to work with teachers to incorporate library materials and skills into the subject curriculums, to keep abreast of new technologies that benefit her or his school or library, and to work with children providing reference service, reading guidance, and other programs of interest. We are now able to provide information that is broader, more in-depth, and more current than ever before. As we embrace this technology we truly become professionals and can lead our teachers, administrators, and students into the twenty-first century.

Notes

1. Michael Gorman, "Thinking the Unthinkable: A Synergetic Profession," *American Libraries* 13 (July/August 1982): 473–474.

2. Walt Crawford, *MARC for Library Use: Understanding Integrated USMARC,* 2d ed. (Boston: G. K. Hall, 1989), 264–265.

Bibliography

Automation for School Libraries: How to Do It from Those Who Have Done It. Chicago: American Library Association, 1994.

Berger, Pam, and Susan K. Kinnell. "Educational CD-ROMs: A Progress Report for the Disc-interested." *School Library Journal* 40, no. 10 (October 1994): 26–31.

Bruce, Harry. "Media Center Automation: A Watershed for the School Library Media Specialist." *School Library Media Quarterly* 22, no. 4 (Summer 1994): 206–212.

Eisenberg, Michael B. "Technology and the Library Media Program: Focus on Potential and Purpose." *School Library Media Quarterly* 18, no. 3 (Spring 1990): 139–141.

Morrill, Martha. "Roles 2000: How to Contain an Ever-Expanding Job." *School Library Journal* 41, no. 1 (January 1995): 32–34.

Murphy, Catherine. "Questions to Guide Retrospective Conversion Choices for School Library Media Centers." *School Library Media Quarterly* 18, no. 2 (Winter 1990): 79–81.

Skapura, Robert. "A Primer on Automating the Card Catalog." *School Library Media Quarterly* 18, no. 2 (Winter 1990): 75–78.

14

MARC and ISBD
Vital Links between Students and Library Materials

Virginia M. Berringer

MARC

In the late 1950s, the Library of Congress (LC) began to investigate the possibility of automating some of its massive cataloging and records maintenance processes. By the fall of 1966, a pilot project was in place and LC began distribution of bibliographic records for English-language monographs to test the feasibility of distributing bibliographic data in machine-readable format to other libraries. This project, supported by a grant from the Council on Library Resources, was called MARC, an acronym for *MA*chine-*R*eadable *C*ataloging. The pilot project, involving LC and 16 participating libraries, resulted in the introduction of the first of the MARC formats, the MARC format for books. This was followed during the 1970s by the introduction of individual MARC formats for serials, scores, sound recordings, audiovisual materials, maps, manuscripts, and machine-readable data files, each using the same basic structure as the format for printed monographs but including identifiers for the unique features of materials in each category. This arbitrary division of library materials based upon publication format made it impossible to adequately record information for many types of materials, such as serials issued in nonprint formats, publications that combine materials in various formats (such as interactive multimedia packages), and print materials accompanied by computer discs, sound recordings, or videos. To rectify these problems and improve access to all data, format integration was initiated and by January 1996 had successfully been adopted, resulting in the elimination of a number of redundant fields and the validation of all tags for use in describing any materials for which they are applicable.

In the 30 years since the introduction of MARC for English language monograph records at LC, MARC has become an international framework for recording, storing, indexing, retrieving, manipulating, and sharing bibliographic data among libraries in nearly every part of the world. It is the basis for huge international databases, such as OCLC and RLIN, and the storage medium for the holdings of libraries in small communities and schools. MARC is everywhere, and has appeared in many variations as other countries have developed systems to fit their own cataloging and communications needs and practices. Unfortunately, the proliferation of distinctive national MARC formats makes it difficult or even impossible for systems designed to store and interpret one format to make sense of records stored according to another set of codes. The development of the ISO 2709 standard has increased the compatibility of developing formats, and there are numerous projects now underway to decrease communication difficulties between national formats. A joint project by the Library of Congress, the British Library, and the National Libraries of Canada and Australia is examining ways to eliminate conflicts in coding among their national formats. Another project, funded by the Commission of the European Communities, is charged with developing a conversion format capable of converting records from one MARC format to any other (UseMARCON).[1]

In addition to the USMARC format for bibliographic records developed primarily by the Library of Congress, USMARC formats have been developed for authority records, holdings records, classification, and community information.

MARC Structure for Recording Information

A MARC bibliographic record involves three elements: the record structure, the content designation, and the data content.[2]

The record begins with information traditionally found in a library catalog. This includes descriptive elements, such as title, edition, publication information, physical description, and notes. These elements as well as access points (series, main and added entries, subject headings, and classification) are defined by national and international standards, including *AACR2,* the ISBDs, *Library of Congress Subject Headings, Sears List of Subject Headings,* and the Dewey and the Library of Congress classification schedules. This information, providing description of and access to library material, is defined in the *USMARC Format for Bibliographic Data* as the data content of the record.

Each element of bibliographic information in the data content is then assigned an identifying code that enables a computer to identify, store, and manipulate it as determined by its programming. This system of content designation is defined in the USMARC format for each category of data to be recorded.

The content of the record and its content designations are fitted into the structure of the record. The record structure for USMARC is based on the American National Standard for Bibliographic Information Interchange (ANSI Z39.2).[3]

The appearance of online displays or output of bibliographic information varies greatly from one system to the next. Just as in typing a catalog card, system designers can determine which information goes where and how much information to include in a display. Thus, a library may choose to display only a few elements of the bibliographic record in its circulation or acquisitions functions, while displaying the full record to patrons. This is achievable because each element is defined by a unique combination of coding in the MARC record.

In the MARC record, data is grouped into several areas. Most of the data in the *leader* is created by the computer when the record is written to the storage medium. The *directory,* which makes it possible for the computer to locate information in the record by recording the exact location of each element within the record, is also automatically generated.

The *variable fields* are where the data recorded by the cataloging agency reside. There are two types of variable fields: variable control fields and variable data fields. Each variable field is identified by a three-digit numerical tag. These tags are grouped into blocks of fields containing related types of information. The first digit of the tag group identifies the type of data to be found in those fields:

0XX   Control information, identification and
      classification numbers, etc.

1XX Main entries

2XX Titles and title paragraph (title, edition, imprint)

3XX Physical description, etc.

4XX Series statements

5XX Notes

6XX Subject access fields

7XX Added entries other than subject or series; linking fields

8XX Series added entries, etc.

9XX Reserved for local implementation[4]

Within each tag group are often coding conventions that are repeated wherever similar data are recorded. For example, tag 100 indicates a personal name main entry. A personal name used as a subject heading is tagged 600, and a personal name as an added entry would be tagged 700. Fields that contain uniform titles will have 30 as the final two digits of the tag.

The *variable control fields* are numbered 001 through 009. Each of these fields contains either a single piece of information (such as field 001), or the record number, or information in coded form from a list of codes defined for each element in each field. Each element in a coded variable control field is identified by its position in the field. For example, the 007 field contains detailed physical description data for nonprint materials and microforms. The first position in this field represents the general type of media. If the first code is "m," the field describes a motion picture. If it is "s," it describes a sound recording. Each character in the rest of the field provides additional specific information about the item, including its specific type, size, color characteristics, sound characteristics, recording characteristics, and so on, each represented by a single letter of the alphabet as defined for that specific position in that specific field.

For a VHS videorecording the 007 field might look like this:

007 vf cbahos

This gibberish describes the item as: a videorecording (v), on videotape (f), in color (c), in VHS format (b), with sound (a), on the videotape (h), which is 3/4 inch wide (o), in stereo (s).

Additional elements in this field would enable the cataloger to specify sound characteristics, archival factors such as base materials, and so forth. Other variable control fields provide information on the source of the cataloging record, accompanying material, language, audience, dates of publication or production, and other data that can be used to identify the material being cataloged and facilitate its retrieval.

The *variable data fields* contain the information most commonly associated with a catalog record, transcribed or recorded in full-text format. A record will contain as many variable data fields as are necessary to describe the item, each identified by the three-digit tag defined for that type of data. Many of the variable field tags may be repeated as often as necessary to record the data required, as a bibliographic record will often include more than one occurrence of a specific type of information, such as subject headings, series, added entries, notes, and so on.

In addition to the tag for identifying the content of a field, the MARC format also includes two indicator positions at the beginning of each variable data field. These allow for additional instructions to the computer regarding storage, indexing, or display of the content of the field. If these indicators are not needed for a specific field, they are defined as blank. One common use of an indicator is to specify how many characters should be skipped at the beginning of a title field to avoid indexing under an article such as "The" (four nonfiling characters, including the space before the next word) or "An" (three nonfiling characters). Indicators can also be used to control printing or display features, such as automatic printing of notes or creation of access points from coded fields.

Within the variable fields, text that may require special manipulation, indexing, or display instructions are separated by subfield codes. These are two-character codes, defined for each tag, composed of a delimiter (|) and a letter or number. For example, in an entry for a personal name, dates are separated from the name portion of the entry by a delimiter and the letter *d*. This makes it possible to write programming to manipulate and display data in a manner that makes sense, separating the name portion of the heading from other elements. For example, the heading for Rembrandt used as a main entry would look like this in the MARC record:

> 100 10 Rembrandt Harmenszoon van Rijn, |d 1606–1669.

As with tags, subfield codes are usually the same for where the same type of information is used for a different purpose in the record. Providing subject access for a book on Rembrandt would require a field tagged 600:

600 10 Rembrandt Harmenszoon van Rijn, |d 1606–1669.

Learning to create and use MARC bibliographic records is an important step in opening your library to the world. The information included in the record comes from the same sources catalogers have always used to provide access to their collections. Information is transcribed from the material being cataloged according to current cataloging rules and standards. Access points are selected, subject headings assigned, and a classification determined—all using the same resources used for creating manual records. Recording this data in a MARC record requires only a knowledge of the basic structure of a MARC record, access to appropriate software, and a copy of the format documentation.[5]

Creation of the bibliographic record using MARC coding is only the beginning. Once a database of MARC records is created, it may be used to provide access to bibliographic materials through the generation of printed card or book catalogs, or computer output microforms, in addition to online and other forms of electronic catalogs. The records can also be contributed to shared bibliographic databases where they may be used by thousands of libraries and their patrons. MARC records generate the catalog cards vendors supply, and the cards libraries purchase from the Library of Congress or from a bibliographic utility. MARC records make it possible for students of all ages to access information quickly and accurately. Figures 1 and 2 show examples of MARC records.

Figure 1. Example of MARC Record

B21542302	Last updated: 02–12–97	Created: 02–12–97	Revision: 1

01	LANG: eng	03 LOCATION: bc	05 BIB LVL: m	07 SUPPRESS: –
02	SKIP: 0	04 CAT DA: 02–12–97	06 MAT TYPE: a	08 COUNTRY: nyu
09	001	32856299		
10	003	OCoLC		
11	005	19970212172252.0		
12	008	950629s1995 nyua j 001 0beng pam a		
13	010	95034387 /AC		
14	020	0872263177		
15	040	DLC | cDLC		
16	041 1	eng | hita		
17	049	AKRR		
18	050 00	ND653.R4 | bP3913 1995		
19	082 00	759.9492 | 220		

(continued)

Figure 1.   (continued)

20	100	1	Pescio, Claudio
21	240	10	Rembrandt e l'Olanda del XVII secolo. | 1English
22	245	10	Rembrandt and seventeenth-century Holland / | cClaudio Pescio ; illustrated by Sergio ; [English translation, Simon Knight]
23	246	1	| iSubtitle on cover: | athe Dutch nation and its painters
24	246	3	Rembrandt and 17th-century Holland
25	260		New York : | bP. Bedrick Books, | c1995
26	300		64 p. : | bcol. ill. ; | c36 cm
27	490	1	Masters of art
28	500		Includes index
29	520		Examines the life and art of Rembrandt against the historical, political, and religious background of the period
30	600	10	Rembrandt Harmenszoon van Rijn, | d1606–1669 | xJuvenile literature
31	600	11	Rembrandt Harmenszoon van Rijn, | d1606–1669
32	650	0	Painters | zNetherlands | xBiography | xJuvenile literature
33	650	1	Artists
34	650	1	Painting, Dutch
35	650	1	Art appreciation
36	651	0	Netherlands | xCivilization | y17th century | xJuvenile literature
37	651	0	Netherlands | xSocial life and customs | xJuvenile literature
38	651	1	Netherlands | xCivilization | y17th century
39	700	1	Rembrandt Harmenszoon van Rijn, | d1606–1669
40	700	0	S {226} ergio
41	830	0	Masters of art (Peter Bedrick Books)

Figure 2.   Example of MARC Record

B21542363	Last updated: 02-12-97 Created: 02-12-97 Revision: 1		
01 LANG: eng	03 LOCATION: bc	05 BIB LVL: m	07 SUPPRESS: –
02 SKIP: 0	04 CAT DA: 02-12-97	06 MAT TYPE: a	08 COUNTRY: cau
09	001	32924645	
10	003	OCoLC	
11	005	19970212174659.0	
12	008	950726s1996 caua j 000 0beng cam a	
13	010	95032105 /AC	
14	019	34883437	
15	020	0152012672	
16	040	DLC | cDLC	

```
17  043     n-us---
18  049     AKRR
19  050  00 GV1061.15.R83 | bK78 1996
20  082  00 796.42 / 092 | aB | 220
21  100  1  Krull, Kathleen
22  245  10 Wilma unlimited : | bhow Wilma Rudolph became the
            world's fastest woman / | cKathleen Krull ; illustrated by
            David Diaz
23  250     1st ed
24  260     San Diego : | bHarcourt Brace, | cc1996
25  300     1 v. (unpaged) : | bcol. ill. ; | c23 x 29 cm
26  520     A biography of the African-American woman who
            overcame crippling polio as a child to become the first
            woman to win three gold medals in track in a single
            Olympics
27  600  10 Rudolph, Wilma, | d1940- | xJuvenile literature
28  600  11 Rudolph, Wilma, | d1940-
29  650  0  Runners (Sports) | zUnited States | xBiography |
            xJuvenile literature
30  650  1  Track and field athletes
31  650  1  Afro-Americans | xBiography
32  650  1  Women | xBiography
33  700  1  Diaz, David, | eill
```

ISBD

Another set of letters that appears frequently in any discussion of library automation and international exchange of bibliographic information is ISBD. This acronym for *I*nternational *S*tandard *B*ibliographic *D*escription represents a set of standards for the creation of bibliographic records that includes both content specifications and formatting requirements.

Developed by the International Federation of Library Associations and Institutions (IFLA), the ISBD(G) or General ISBD was first published in 1977.[6] The primary purposes of the ISBDs are to make records from different sources interchangeable, to assist in the interpretation of bibliographic records regardless of the language of the content, and to aid in the conversion of bibliographic records to machine-readable form.[7]

The ISBD identifies the elements of description and specifies the order in which these elements are to appear in the bibliographic description (if applicable to the item being cataloged). ISBD mandates the punctuation used to separate elements of the description and identifies the chief sources of information to be used for recording each element of the bibliographic description. These elements of description, order of the elements, and prescribed punctuation have been incorporated into the *Anglo-American Cataloguing Rules.* The structure of MARC records is also based on the ISBD(G) and the specialized ISBDs established for each type of material.

ISBD defines eight areas of information to be included in a bibliographic description:

1. Title and statement of responsibility area

2. Edition area

3. Material (or type of publication) specific area

4. Publication, distribution, etc. area

5. Physical description area

6. Series area

7. Note area

8. Standard number (or alternative) and terms of availability area[8]

ISBD deals strictly with the descriptive aspect of creating a bibliographic record. In the eight areas defined by ISBD there is no mention of access points. Choice of entry, form of entry, and other access points (such as subject and classification) are left to the cataloging rules and guidelines established by the library communities creating the records. In the Anglo-American community, the principles and structure of the ISBD have become important parts of the creation of today's machine-readable bibliographic records through the use of AACR2 and MARC.

Notes

1. Fernanda M. Campos, M. Ines Lopes, and Rosa M. Galvao, "MARC Formats and Their Use: An Overview," *Program* 29, no. 4 (October 1995): 445.

2. *USMARC Format for Bibliographic Data* (Washington, D.C.: Cataloging Distribution Service, Library of Congress, 1994–), Introduction, 1.

3. Walt Crawford, *MARC for Library Use: Understanding Integrated USMARC,* 2d ed. (Boston: G. K. Hall, 1989), 32.

4. *USMARC Format for Bibliographic Data,* Introduction, 4.

5. *USMARC Format for Bibliographic Data: Including Guidelines for Content Designation,* prepared by the Network Development and MARC Standards Office of the Library of Congress, "defines the codes and conventions (tags, indicators, subfield codes, and coded values) that identify the data elements in USMARC bibliographic records. This document is intended for the use of personnel involved in the creation and maintenance of bibliographic records, as well as those involved in the design and maintenance of systems for communication and processing of bibliographic records." (Introduction, 1)

6. International Federation of Library Associations and Institutions, Working Group on the General International Standard Bibliographic Description, *ISBD(G): General International Standard Bibliographic Description: Annotated Text* (London: IFLA International Office for UBC, 1977).

7. Ibid., 1.

8. Ibid., 2–3.

15

Curriculum-Enhanced MARC

Catherine Murphy

USERS OF SCHOOL LIBRARIES and teacher resource centers often have problems in accessing curriculum materials in card catalogs as well as in online catalogs. Some of the data, such as a curriculum objective or indicators of the suitability of the material for a particular subject or class, can have a direct bearing on the effectiveness of instruction and learning. Other information will be equally important to any catalog searcher, such as a review of the material and its appropriateness for specific audiences. Some information, notably the appropriate age or grade for the user of this material, is often found in USMARC records available from many sources, but not consistently. The more detailed and specific data, such as a learning objective for a particular subject and grade level ("Texas Math Objective 1 read number words"), audience characteristics (special education, honors or advanced classes, low motivation levels), and even reviews, have been entered locally in an inconsistent manner, or are just not available.

The new curriculum-enhanced features of the MARC format recently approved by the Library of Congress address the problems that catalog users encounter as they search for specific learning materials. There is now a standard style for entering curriculum information in a bibliographic record, published for the first time in the 1994 edition of the USMARC Bibliographic Formats.[1] The curriculum enhancements include new locations for a review in the 520 field, new indicators for audience characteristics in the 521 field, and a new field for curriculum objectives, 658. Other data elements included in the second level of description of materials, defined in AACR2, and recommended in the Guidelines for Standardized Cataloging of Children's Materials, are incorporated into the new curriculum-enhanced format suggested in the original proposal to the Library of Congress, and also suggested to practitioners.[2] Not all the elements will be appropriate to use in the cataloging of every curriculum support item, but adherence to the general guidelines offers libraries and commercial services the opportunity to provide new enhancements that can be shared across networks because they are standardized. The following sections provide some history, guidelines, and suggestions for implementing the new standards.

History of Cataloging for the Curriculum

The special cataloging needs of students and teachers have received some attention over the years. The Library of Congress Annotated Card Program was developed to provide more specific information about all children's books, including special subject headings, substantial summaries, and audience age and grade levels. Several lists of subject headings that are based on children's interests and vocabulary have been published. The educational focus of the library resource center creates a particular need, however, to link the book or film to a learning situation. As early as 1976 Wehmeyer suggested the computerized linking of educational objectives or vocabulary to catalog records.[3] In 1985, in the early days of online catalog development in school libraries, Murphy found that practitioners responsible for conversion were not as aware of the importance of mainstream catalog standards as they might be, yet these school librarians were finding it important to add special headings for reading and other curriculum units to the converted records.[4]

Probably the best-known local system for individualizing the cataloging of instructional materials, that was later marketed to other schools, is the Annehurst Curriculum Classification System (ACCS).[5] This non-MARC system for individualizing instruction, originally developed for a school in Ohio, is really a forerunner of the new, enhanced MARC format for curriculum materials. ACCS was a numbering system that cross-referenced all kinds of educational materials (including articles in *National Geographic* and *American Heritage* magazines) to different learner styles, interests, and tests. Indexing of magazines is now covered (if not as individualized) by periodical databases, but the profiling of media and books according to their usefulness in classroom situations has not been otherwise available.

It is not too surprising, then, that the initiative for the nationally approved curriculum-enhanced MARC format came from the state of Ohio where ACCS was developed. The state standards committee accommodated a request from school librarians to standardize the location of curriculum information in a catalog record. Roger Minier, director of the Northwest Ohio Technology Foundation (NWOET), led the effort to develop a pilot database of catalog records of audiovisual materials, not only rich in descriptive detail but tagged as support material for test objectives, special classes, and so on.[6] In January 1993, Minier, supported by other colleagues, presented a proposal to the MAchine Readable Bibliographical Information (MARBI) Committee of the American Library Association (ALA) to adopt a national standard based on the INFOhio guidelines for curriculum enhancements. The approval of these guidelines by MARBI and their recommendation for adoption by the Library of Congress has made it possible for different educational agencies as well as commercial services to implement a format that can be shared.

Recommendations for Curriculum-Enhanced MARC Format

It should be noted that these guidelines do not constitute a new format. USMARC is still the format but it has been enhanced with curriculum information. The recommendations for new enhancements cover three tags or fields, 520, 521, and 658. The only new field, 658, is reserved for curriculum objectives, their sources, and the extent of correlation. In the 520 field, the indicator value 1, subfield a, can now contain a review (in quotes) and subfield b, its source. In the 521 tag, other indicators have been added: value 3, subfield a, special audience characteristics (for example, tactile learner), subfield b, its source; and value 4, subfield a, motivation/ interest level (for example, highly motivated), subfield b, its source. As stated earlier, curriculum-enhanced records are expected to include all data elements in other tags to meet the second level of description as defined in AACR2, for the appropriate description of non-print as well as print materials. The current recommendations for a Core record can also incorporate curriculum-enhanced elements.

The following examples of curriculum enhancements (b indicates blank, = indicates delimiter) are derived from examples given in the *USMARC Format Guidelines*.[7] An explanation follows each example in parentheses.

> *Review:* **520 1b** =a"Combines the most frequently asked questions regarding AIDS with the most prominent U.S. physician, former Surgeon General C. Everett Koop, resulting in an informative 38-minute projection."—Cf. Video rating guide for libraries, winter 1990.
>
> (The review should be evaluative and placed in quotes, followed by its source.)
>
> *Audience:* **521 3b** =aAudio impaired=bLENOCA
>
> (This material is suitable for a hearing-impaired student. The agency designating its use is an Ohio educational agency. An acronym for the agency is generally used.)
>
> **521 4b** =aModerately motivated=ahigh interest=bLENOCA
>
> (The audience or class is average in motivation but has a high interest level. The source of the designation is the same agency indicated in the preceding tag. Remember that other audience characteristics are included in values **0** for reading grade level, **1** for interest age level, and **2** for interest grade level.)
>
> *Curr. Obj.* **658 bb** =aHealth objective 1=bhandicapped awareness=cLENOCA=dhighly correlated=2ohco
>
> (The main curriculum objective is Health #1 in an Ohio list; secondary curriculum objective is handicapped awareness. The source is the LENOCA agency. The material is highly correlated to the objective, that is, the con-

tent is mostly about the objective(s) and not just partially so. The subfield 2 contains a USMARC code that identifies the source list from which the index term or code was assigned. Catalogers must use a published list for the source and may submit a new list for coding to the Library of Congress for inclusion in *US Marc Code List for Relators, Sources, Description Conventions.*)

Implementing the Format

You may have begun to hear vendors of cataloging services promoting their records as "curriculum enhanced" or just plain "enhanced." At this point, those terms probably indicate that the 520 and the 521 tags have been enriched. The commercial providers of cataloging services are not concerned with curriculum or test objectives. Perhaps at some point they will pick up on national standards such as those published by the National Council of Teachers of Mathematics. These national standards may be adopted by state education departments and included in 658 fields of catalog records where they may apply to any state's curriculum. More vendors now are responding to a demand for detailed records by adding reviews as well as reading grade level and age and interest levels. If practitioners ask for quality data, including a full physical description, contents notes, teacher guide and other supplementary material information, and so on, the market will be competitive in response to these requests. A conversion of a school catalog is an opportunity to get curriculum and test objectives applied to materials and catalog records and some schools are contracting for this service.

The INFOhio network is a good model for a statewide approach to developing a curriculum-enhanced catalog. If library media specialists from around the state, working with their teachers, can contribute original curriculum-enhanced cataloging for a particular subject collection or format, all the files can be shared. If one school district identifies library materials for a specific curriculum unit (ninth grade social studies, for example), those books and software will be found in the libraries of other members who can benefit from the added information. Some of these correlations can be found in printed curriculum guides that are already available.

Local schools or school districts may have their own unique curricula. All the materials for themes, units, and so forth can be linked to the library's collection as needed. It is important to refer only to published lists for curriculum index terms. School districts may apply to the Library of Congress for a code listing, as suggested earlier. It may become a practice in applying curriculum headings in the 658 field to use national standards where they are available (for example, mathematics) or to use thesauri, such as ERIC for educational terms or the Eisenhower National Clearinghouse for mathematics and science vocabulary, where regular subject headings are inadequate.

Local and state education agencies will have to determine their own cataloging profiles and priorities. Not every data element will be needed. Special education departments will be more concerned with the learner characteristics for disabled populations than will the mainstream groups. If a local or state group coordinates its efforts, a great deal of original data entry can be accomplished. At the same time, cataloging services and automated system vendors must be encouraged to supply the quality data that is available to them. Also, it is not enough to put the information in the catalog record; the system must be able to retrieve and display it. Some system vendors are beginning to do so.

It is hoped that the practitioners in school libraries and resource centers will seek curriculum data enhancements in the market and encourage their state agencies to support the format. In 1995, Roger Minier obtained a grant from the U.S. Office of Education to train library media specialists from around the country in developing curriculum-enhanced records. Two well-attended workshops were held with the stipulation that attendees offer the same training in their home areas. Gradually, the movement is growing and more commercial providers, as well as librarians, are becoming aware of the value of curriculum-enhanced cataloging.

Notes

1. *USMARC Format for Bibliographic Data: Including Guidelines for Content Designation.* Washington, D.C.: Library of Congress, Cataloging Distribution Service, 1994-.

2. "Guidelines for Standardized Cataloging of Children's Materials," in *Cataloging Correctly for Kids: An Introduction to the Tools,* rev. ed.,

ed. Sharon Zuiderveld (Chicago: Resources & Technical Services Division/CCS Cataloging of Children's Materials Committee, American Library Association, 1991).

3. Lillian M. Wehmeyer, "Cataloging the School Media Center as a Specialized Collection," *Library Resources & Technical Services* 20 no. 4 (Fall 1976): 315–325.

4. Catherine Murphy, *Microcomputer Online Public Access Catalogs: Practices and Attitudes of School Library Media Specialists toward Standardization* (Ph.D. diss., Columbia University, 1987).

5. Jack Rimmel Frymier, *Annehurst Curriculum Classification System* (West Lafayette, Ind.: Kappa Delta Pi, 1977).

6. Author's notes from meetings with Roger Minier, NWOET, Bowling Green State University, Bowling Green, Ohio, September 1993–1996.

7. *USMARC Format.*

16

What Is
MicroLIF?

Joycelyn Fobes Brand

MICROLIF (INITIALLY AN ACRONYM for *Micro*computer *Library Interchange Format*), a MAchine-Readable Cataloging (MARC) format, was designed for microcomputers. As originally conceived, it consisted of a communications format without a directory for each record but with bibliographic data that conformed to the *USMARC Format for Bibliographic Data.*

In the 1980s, library circulation software programs for microcomputers gained popularity, especially in schools. The need for bibliographic records for these automated circulation systems was the driving force behind the creation of the MicroLIF format. School libraries were purchasing a microcomputer and the software for a circulation system or an online catalog or both, as well as processed books and diskettes containing bibliographic records. Consequently, vendors of library books and cataloging data serving these libraries communicated with vendors of software programs regarding the requirements for the bibliographic records being used in circulation systems and online catalogs.

Although the USMARC format for bibliographic records was at that time one of the three communications formats defined for use with magnetic tapes, it was difficult to adapt to the microcomputer environment. In response to these difficulties, a group of vendors began a cooperative effort to develop a bibliographic record format that would work well in their customers' microcomputer systems.

As the basis for its record format, this vendor MicroLIF group chose the predecessor of the *USMARC Format for Bibliographic Data,* the *MARC Formats for Bibliographic Data* as defined by the Library of Congress (LC). However, the MicroLIF format did not contain a directory for each record. Rather, the content designators and the content of each record were rearranged to facilitate both the use of these records in the microcomputer environment and the addition of data elements not yet defined by the USMARC format, but needed by school libraries. "A Statement of Purpose," printed by the MicroLIF group on February 3, 1987, stated "the objective is to have a format which can be generated with relative ease from MARC data, can be easily recognized and manipulated by someone familiar with the MARC record layout, and can be used to re-create the original MARC record in MARC communication format whenever necessary."

A bibliographic record in the USMARC format consists of three components. A 24-position leader of "data elements that provide information for the processing of the record" is followed by the directory.[1] The directory is "a series of entries that contain the tag, length, and starting location of each variable field within a record. Each entry is 12 character positions in length."[2] The third element of the record is the variable field area. Those variable fields that contain data have two indicators and a two-character subfield code.

As initially conceived, the MicroLIF format consisted of a content designator or tag, its two indicators, the initial subfield code with the corresponding data, any additional subfield codes with the corresponding data required to complete the field, and a field terminator consisting of a carriage return and possibly a line feed. The sequence of the tags and data followed the USMARC format. The first tag of every bibliographic record in the MicroLIF format was the leader, which was denoted as LDR. As previously stated, the element common to USMARC records that was missing in a MicroLIF record was the directory. However, computer programs were developed that could re-create the directory if the need existed to transfer a MicroLIF record into a USMARC record.

Some of the data elements needed by school libraries, but not defined by the USMARC format as it existed in the mid-1980s, included local call number, bar-code number, ship to account number, list price, book vendor control number, book vendor tin or bin number, and the order quantity. These additional data elements were part of the MicroLIF record as tags 900 through 906, respectively.

Because elements of a bibliographic record in the USMARC format are at best difficult to decipher, the record is often displayed in a format similar to that of the MicroLIF record. That is, each tag with its indicators followed by the subfield code(s) and corresponding data is displayed as a new line of the bibliographic record. An example of the same bibliographic record for *Where's the Baby?* by Pat Hutchins in the MicroLIF and the USMARC formats illustrates this difference. Figure 1 shows the MicroLIF format; Figure 2 shows the USMARC format.

As librarians have become more knowledgeable about the entire process of creating automated bibliographic records, and as hardware and software have become more sophisticated, the need has increased to eliminate differences between the USMARC format and the MicroLIF format. In order to adopt the USMARC format while continuing to meet the needs of the microcomputer environment and its users, the MicroLIF group began working within the framework of the American Library Association's interdivisional committee on machine-readable bibliographic information (MARBI),

Figure 1. A Record in the MicroLIF Format

```
LDR00514nam 22002411 4500^
001CCC89231785^
00519901106000000.0^
008901106    a j   0 0 eng d^
010 _a 86033566 ^
040 _aCatalog Card Company^
08214_aE^
10010_aHutchins, Pat.^
24510_aWhere's the baby?^
2600 _bGreenwillow_c1988.^
300  _aunp_billus.^
520   _aWhen Grandma, Ma, and Hazel Monster want to find Baby
Monster, they follow the messy trail he has left. ^
650 7_aMonsters_xFiction_2sears^
650 7_aInfants_xFiction_2sears^
650 7_aCleanliness_xFiction_2sears^
900 _aE Hut^
901 _a4874^
903 _a11.88^
906 _a01^
```

Figure 2. A Record in the USMARC Format

```
      00669nam   22002411   45000010012000000050017000 1
2008004100029010001700070040002200087082000600109100001
9001152450022001342600023001563000016001795200108001956
5000290030365000280033265000320036090000090039290100090
0401903001000410906000700420    86033566
19890613000000.0 890613
      a j   0 0 eng d a 86033566    aCatalog Card Corp  14 aE
10 aHutchins, Pat. 1 aWhere's the baby? 0 bGreenwillow
c1988. aunp billus. aWhen Grandma, Ma, and Hazel Monster
want to find Baby Monster, they follow the messy trail he has
left. 7 aMonsters xFiction 2sears 7 aInfants xFiction 2sears
7 aCleanliness xFiction 2sears   aE Hu   a4874   a11.88   a01
```

which is the advisory group to LC regarding modifications to the USMARC format.

Consequently, the MicroLIF format was revised in 1990 for implementation in 1991. The revisions included the use of the USMARC format with a leader and record directory for each bibliographic record and the replacement of the 9XX tags for local data with tag 852 and its multiple subfields for local data from the *USMARC Format for Holdings Data.*

In addition to the revised format for the bibliographic record, two label files are included on the diskette. These two files communicate information from the originating system to the receiving system, such as the name of the system compiling the bibliographic records, the date the records were compiled, and the number of bibliographic records on the diskette.

Microcomputer users of bibliographic records have a choice of the format defined in the 1980s and referred to as the "MicroLIF" format or the newer format utilizing the 852 tag for local data and referred to as the "USMARC/852 Holdings Data" format shown in Figure 3.

The MicroLIF group submitted four new variable fields needed in the microcomputer environment, especially in the school library, to MARBI for consideration. These four data fields were approved and have been added to the *USMARC Format for Bibliographic Data.*The new fields consist of three note fields: citation/references note (tag 510) for citations or references that specify where an item has been cited or reviewed; target audience note (tag 521) for

Figure 3. A Record in the USMARC/852 Holdings Data Format

```
        00792nam 2200241 a
45000010012000000005001700012008004100029010002000070020
00150009002000150010504000350012005000240015508200100001
79100001900189245004200208260003600250300003700286526001
08003236500030004316500029004616500033004908520000
2700523-CCE96204083-19960823110813.0-960823
s1988  nyua b  000 1 eng          d-        a 86033566 /AC-
a0688059333- -a0688059341- aDLCcDLCdCatalog Card
Company-00aPZ7.H96165bWh 1988-00aE220-1 -aHutchins,
Pat.-10aWhere's the baby? /cby Pat Hutchins.- aNew York
:bGreenwillow,c1988.- -aunp. :bcol. ill. ;c21 x 26 cm.- aWhen
Grandma, Ma, and Hazel Monster want to find Baby Monster, they
follow the messy trail he has left.- 7aMonstersxFiction.2sears-
7aInfantsxFiction.2sears-    7aCleanlinessxFiction.2sears-1
hEiHup4874 9P11.88usd-_
```

reading grade level, interest age level, or interest grade level; and awards note (tag 586) for information on awards conferred upon the item. The fourth variable field that has been added to the USMARC formats is an index term-uncontrolled field (tag 653) containing terms not derived from a controlled subject heading system or thesaurus.

In 1995, the vendor group working with the MicroLIF community found its role changing to one of disseminating information to MARBI, microcomputer library users, and the library community at large. Consequently, the group redefined the MicroLIF acronym from *Micro*computer *L*ibrary *I*nterchange *F*ormat to *Micro*computer *L*ibrary *I*nformation *F*orum.

Future plans for the MicroLIF group include continued participation in MARBI as U.S., Canadian, and British representatives work to create one uniform MARC format, possibly to be named IMARC. Another goal of the MicroLIF group is the continuing coordination and representation of the needs of microcomputer library users, especially school libraries, with library groups such as MARBI and the library community. And, as the new meaning for the acronym MicroLIF implies, the dissemination of information to all who need it is an essential function of the MicroLIF vendor group.

Notes

1. *USMARC Format for Bibliographic Data* (Washington, D.C.: Library of Congress, 1988), 3.
2. Ibid.

Bibliography

Avram, Henriette D. *MARC, Its History and Implications.* Washington, D.C.: Library of Congress, 1975.

Byrne, Deborah J. *MARC Manual: Understanding and Using MARC Records.* Englewood, Colo.: Libraries Unlimited, 1991.

Crawford, Walt. *MARC for Library Use: Understanding Integrated USMARC.* 2d ed. Boston: G. K. Hall, 1989.

Hagler, Ronald. *The Bibliographic Record and Information Technology.* 3d ed. Chicago: American Library Association, 1997.

U.S. Library of Congress. Automated Systems Office. *MARC Formats for Bibliographic Data.* Washington, D.C.: Library of Congress, 1980.

USMARC Format for Bibliographic Data. Washington, D.C.: Library of Congress, 1988.

USMARC Format for Bibliographic Data. Washington, D.C.: Library of Congress, 1994.

USMARC Format for Holdings Data. Washington, D.C.: Library of Congress, 1989.

The USMARC Formats: Background and Principles. Washington, D.C.: Library of Congress, 1989.

Bibliography

Kathleen Wheatley

"Primary Tools" includes tools needed to catalog and classify a library collection. "Cataloging for Children" contains journal articles and books that will assist those who catalog children's materials. Although previous editions of this book attempted to be all-inclusive, the focus of this bibliography is to be more a practical tool. "Further Reading and Study" includes books and articles suggested for further reading, with an emphasis on current materials.

Primary Tools

Descriptive Cataloging

Anglo-American Cataloguing Rules. 2d ed., 1988 rev. Edited by Michael Gorman and Paul W. Winkler. Chicago: American Library Association, 1988.

Gorman, Michael. *The Concise AACR2, 1988 Revision.* Chicago: American Library Association, 1989.

Classification

Association for Library Collections and Technical Services. Interactive Multimedia Guidelines Review Task Force. *Guidelines for Bibliographic Description of Interactive Multimedia.* Chicago: American Library Association, 1994.

Chan, Lois Mai. *Cataloging and Classification: An Introduction.* 2d ed. New York: McGraw-Hill, 1993.

Dewey, Melvil. *Abridged Dewey Decimal Classification and Relative Index.* Edited by Joan S. Mitchell, Julianne Beall, Winton E. Matthews Jr., and Gregory R. New. 13th ed. Albany, N.Y.: OCLC Forest Press, 1997.

———. *Dewey Decimal Classification and Relative Index.* Edited by Joan S. Mitchell, Julianne Beall, Winton E. Matthews Jr., and Gregory R. New. 21st ed. Albany, N.Y.: OCLC Forest Press, 1996.

Howarth, Lynne. *AACR2 Decisions and Rule Interpretations.* 5th ed. Ottawa, Ont.: Canadian Library Association, 1991.

Library of Congress. Subject Cataloging Division. *Library of Congress Classification Schedules.* 10th ed. Washington, D.C.: Library of Congress, 1986.

Olson, Nancy B., ed. *Cataloging of Internet Resources: A Manual and Practical Guide.* http://www.oclc.org/oclc/man/9256cat/tcc.htm

Taylor, Arlene G. *Cataloging with Copy: A Decision-Maker's Handbook.* 2d ed. Englewood, Colo.: Libraries Unlimited, 1988.

USMARC Format for Bibliographic Data. Washington, D.C.: Library of Congress, 1994.

Subject Headings

Library of Congress. *Children's Literature Catalog.* Washington, D.C.: Library of Congress, 1986. Microfiche.

Library of Congress. Subject Cataloging Division. *Library of Congress Subject Headings.* 19th ed. Washington, D.C.: Library of Congress, 1996.

National Library of Canada. *Canadian Subject Headings.* 3d ed. Edited by Alina Schweitzer. Ottawa, Ont.: Canada Communication Group, 1992.

Sears List of Subject Headings. 16th ed. Edited by Joseph Miller. New York: H. W. Wilson, 1997.

Sears List of Subject Headings: Canadian Companion. 5th ed. Edited by Lynne Lighthall. New York: H. W. Wilson, 1995.

Sears: Lista de Encabezamientos de Materia. Translated by Carmen Rovira. New York: H. W. Wilson, 1984.

Subject Headings for Children: A List of Subject Headings Used by Library of Congress with Dewey Numbers Added. Edited by Lois Winkel. 2 vol. Albany, N.Y.: OCLC Forest Press, 1997.

Wynar, Bohdan S. *Introduction to Cataloging and Classification.* 8th ed. Edited by Arlene G. Taylor. Littleton, Colo.: Libraries Unlimited, 1992.

Filing

ALA Filing Rules. Chicago: American Library Association, 1980.

Library of Congress Filing Rules. Prepared by John C. Rather and Susan C. Biebel. Washington, D.C.: Library of Congress, 1980.

Cataloging for Children

Association for Library Collections & Technical Services, Cataloging of Children's Materials Committee. "Cataloging for Children: A Selective Bibliography." *ACLTS Newsletter* 1, no. 4 (1990): 40–41.

Automating School Library Catalogs: A Reader. Edited by Catherine Murphy. Englewood, Colo.: Libraries Unlimited, 1992.

Automation for School Libraries: How to Do It from Those Who Have Done It. Chicago: American Library Association, 1994.

Berman, Sanford. "Children, 'Idiots,' the 'Underground,' and Others." *Library Journal* 96, no. 22 (December 15, 1971): 4162-4167.

———. "Juvenalia." In *Joy of Cataloging: Essays, Letters, Reviews, and Other Explosions,* edited by Sanford Berman, 158-165. Phoenix: Oryx Press, 1981.

———. "The Terrible Truth about Teenlit Cataloging." *Top of the News* 43, no. 3 (Spring 1987): 311-320.

Bocher, Robert. "MITINET: Catalog Conversion to a MARC Database (in Wisconsin School Libraries)." *School Library Media Quarterly* 31, no. 7 (March 1985): 109-112.

Bruce, Harry. "Media Center Automation: A Watershed for the School Library Media Specialist." *School Library Media Quarterly* 22, no. 4 (Summer 1994): 206-212.

Busey, Paula, and Tom Doerr. "Kid's Catalog: An Information Retrieval System for Children." *Journal of Youth Services in Libraries* 7, no. 1 (Fall 1993): 77-84.

Byrne, Deborah J. *MARC Manual: Understanding and Using MARC Records.* Englewood, Colo.: Libraries Unlimited, 1991.

Carothers, Diane Foxhill. *Self-Instruction Manual for Filing Catalog Cards.* Washington, D.C.: Library of Congress, 1981.

Chan, Lois Mai. "Further Comments on the Cataloging of Children's Materials." *Unabashed Librarian,* no. 14 (Winter 1975): 14-15.

———. "The Tenth Abridged Dewey Decimal Classification . . . and Children's Room/School Library Collections." *Library Journal* 98, no. 16 (September 15, 1973): 2620-2625.

Chan, Lois Mai, John P. Comaromi, Joan S. Mitchell, and Mohinder Satija. *Dewey Decimal Classification: A Practical Guide.* 2d ed., rev. for DDC 21. Albany, N.Y.: OCLC Forest Press, 1996.

Chapman, Liz. *How to Catalogue: A Practical Handbook Using AACR2 and Library of Congress.* 2d ed. London: Clive Bingley, 1990; distributed by the American Library Association.

Children's Catalog. 17th ed. New York: H. W. Wilson, 1996.

Culberg, Laura. "Using LC Classification for Children's Materials." *RTSD Newsletter* 12, no. 4 (Fall 1987): 46-48.

DeHart, Florence E., and Marylouise D. Meder. "Cataloging Children's Materials: A Stage of Transition." In *Cataloging Special Materials:*

Critiques and Innovations, edited by Sanford Berman, 71–97. Phoenix: Oryx Press, 1986.

———. "Piaget, Picture Storybooks, and Subject Access." *Technicalities* 5, no. 3 (March 1985): 3–5, 16.

DeHart, Florence E., and Ellen Searles. "Developmental Values as Catalog Access Points for Children's Fiction." *Technicalities* 5, no. 1 (January 1985): 13–15.

Downing, Mildred H. *Introduction to Cataloging and Classification.* 6th ed. Jefferson, N.C.: McFarland, 1992.

Duncan, Winifred E. "LC's National Standard for Cataloging Children's Materials: Implementation." *School Library Journal* 22, no. 5 (January 1976): 21, 23.

Eisenberg, Michael B. "Technology and the Library Media Program: Focus on Potential and Purpose." *School Library Media Quarterly* 18, no. 3 (Spring 1990): 139–141.

"Guidelines for Standardized Cataloging of Children's Materials." *Top of the News* 40, no.1 (Fall 1983): 49–55.

Harris, Jessica L., and Theodore C. Hines. "LC Cataloging as a Standard for Children's Materials." *Library Journal* 97, no. 22 (15 December 1972): 4052–4054.

Hennepin County Library. *Children's Information Needs: Unique Subject Access in Hennepin County Library.* Minnetonka, Minn.: Hennepin County Library, 1985.

Hill, Donna. *The Picture File: A Manual and a Curriculum-Related Subject Heading List.* 2d ed. Hamden, Conn.: Linnet Books, 1978.

Hines, Patricia S. "Addendum to Article on Library of Congress Annotated Cards for Children's Literature." *Library Resources & Technical Services* 10 (Fall 1966): 457–460.

Hines, Theodore C., and Lois Winkel. "A New Information Access Tool for Children's Media." *Library Resources & Technical Services* 27, no. 1 (January/March 1983): 94–104.

Hines, Theodore C., Lois Winkel, and Roseann Collins. "The Children's Media Data Bank." *Top of the News* 36, no. 2 (Winter 1980): 176–180.

Hooten, Patricia A. "Online Catalogs: Will They Improve Children's Access?" *Journal of Youth Services in Libraries* 2, no. 3 (Spring 1989): 267–272.

Hunter, Eric J. *An Introduction to AACR2: A Programmed Guide to the Second Edition of the Anglo-American Cataloguing Rules, 1988 Revision.* London: Clive Bingley, 1989; distributed by the American Library Association.

Intner, Sheila S., and Jean Weihs. *Standard Cataloging for School and Public Libraries.* 2d ed. Englewood, Colo.: Libraries Unlimited, 1996.

Jacobson, Frances F. "From Dewey to Mosaic: Considerations in Interface Design for Children." *Internet Research* 5, no. 2 (1995): 67–73.

Koger, Ellen. "Subject Headings for Children's Fiction." *Technical Services Quarterly* 2, no. 1/2 (Fall/Winter 1984): 13–18.

Levitt, Jent G. "Cataloging for Children." *Unabashed Librarian,* no. 19 (Spring 1976): 15–16.

Lewis, Roberta Welsh. "Elementary School Children Express Their Need for Catalog Information." *Journal of Youth Services in Libraries* 2, no. 2 (Winter 1989): 151–156.

Lima, Carolyn W., and John A. Lima. *A to Zoo: Subject Access to Children's Picture Books.* 4th ed. New Providence, N.J.: Bowker, 1993.

McDonald, Frances M. "Information Access for Youth: Issues and Concerns." *Library Trends* 37, no. 1 (Summer 1988): 28–42.

Middle and Junior High School Library Catalog. 7th ed. Edited by Anne Price and Juliette Yaakov. New York: H. W. Wilson, 1995.

Miller, Rosalind E., and Jane C. Terwillegar. *Commonsense Cataloging: A Cataloger's Manual.* 4th ed., rev. New York: H. W. Wilson, 1990.

Murphy, Catherine. "Questions to Guide Retrospective Conversion Choices for School Library Media Centers." *School Library Media Quarterly* 18, no. 2 (Winter 1990): 79–81.

O'Grady, Marina. "CACL [Canadian Association of Children's Librarians] Studies Subject Heading Use in Canadian Books." *Feliciter* 29, no. 11 (November 1983): 4.

Ozaki, Hiroko. *Subject Headings and Subject Access to Children's Literature: A Bibliography Covering Materials Issues 1975–1985.* Ottawa, Ont.: National Library of Canada, Library Documentation Centre, 1986.

Perkins, John W. "An Adapted Library of Congress Classification for Children's Materials." *Library Resources & Technical Services* 22, no. 2 (Spring 1978): 174–178.

———. *Library of Congress Classification Adapted for Children's Books.* 2d ed. Inglewood, Calif.: Inglewood Public Library, 1972.

Roman, Susan. "Online Catalogs and Specialized Clienteles: Children and Youth." In *Human Aspects of Library Automation: Helping Staff and Patrons Cope,* edited by Debora Shaw, 94–100. Urbana: University of Illinois Graduate School of Library and Information Science, 1986.

Rose, Lois Doman. "LC's National Standard for Cataloging Children's Materials: Explanation." *School Library Journal* 22, no. 5 (January 1976): 20, 22.

Skapura, Robert. "A Primer on Automating the Card Catalog." *School Library Media Quarterly* 18, no. 2 (Winter 1990): 75–78.

Taylor, Audrey. "PRECIS Indexing in School Libraries: A Tool for Tomorrow Today." In *Sharing: A Challenge for All,* edited by John G. Wright, 372–384. Kalamazoo, Mich.: International Association of School Librarianship, School of Librarianship, Western Michigan University, 1982.

Truett, Carol. "AACR Who? The Case for Using the New Anglo-American Cataloguing Rules in the School Library Media Center." *School Library Media Quarterly* 12, no. 1 (Fall 1983): 38–43.

Vita, Susan. "Getting More CIP in the Center: A Look at the Value of CIP for School Library Media Centers." *School Library Media Quarterly* 13, no. 1 (Winter 1985): 41–43.

Wehmeyer, Lillian M. "Cataloging the School Media Center as a Specialized Collection." *Library Resources & Technical Services* 20, no. 4 (Fall 1976): 315–325.

Woods, William E. *Manual and List of Subject Headings Used on the Woods Cross Reference Cards.* 6th ed. Evergreen Park, Ill.: Woods Library Pub. Co., 1987.

Yonkers Public Library. *Children's Services. A Guide to Subjects and Concepts in Picture Book Format.* 2d ed. Dobbs Ferry, N.Y.: Oceana, 1979.

Further Reading and Study

Adcock, Donald C. *Guidelines for Cataloging Microcomputer Software.* Chicago: American Association of School Libraries, 1987.

Akers, Susan Grey. *Akers' Simple Library Cataloging.* 7th ed, completely revised and rewritten by Arthur Curley and Jana Varlejs. Metuchen, N.J.: Scarecrow Press, 1984.

American Library Association, Resources and Technical Services Division. Subject Analysis Committee. *Guidelines on Subject Access to Microcomputer Software.* Chicago: American Library Association, 1986.

"Annotated Card Program: AC Subject Headings." In *Library of Congress Subject Headings,* 19th ed., xix–xxxvi. Washington D.C.: Library of Congress Cataloging Policy and Support Division, 1996.

Applebaum, Edmond L. "Library of Congress Annotated Cards for Children's Literature." *Library Resourcses & Technical Services* 10 (Fall 1966): 455–457.

Avram, Henriette D. *MARC, Its History and Implications.* Washington, D.C.: Library of Congress, 1975.

Borgman, Christine L. "Why Are Online Catalogs Still Hard to Use?" *Journal of the American Society for Information Science* 47, no. 7 (July 1996): 493–503.

Borgman, Christine L., Sandra G. Hirsh, and Virginia A. Walter. "Children's Searching Behavior on Browsing and Keyword Online Catalogs: The Science Library Catalog Project." *Journal of the American Society for Information Science* 46, no. 9 (October 1995): 663–684.

Campos, Fernanda M., M. Ines Lopes, and Rosa M. Galvao. "MARC Formats and Their Use: An Overview." *Program* 29, no. 4 (October 1995): 445–459.

Chan, Lois Mai. *Immroth's Guide to the Library of Congress Classification.* 4th ed. Littleton, Colo.: Libraries Unlimited, 1990.

———. *Library of Congress Subject Headings: Principles and Application.* 3d ed. Englewood, Colo.: Libraries Unlimited, 1995.

Chan, Lois Mai, John P. Comaromi, Joan S. Mitchell, and Mohinder Satija. *Dewey Decimal Classification: A Practical Guide.* 2d ed., rev. for DDC 21. Albany, N.Y.: OCLC Forest Press, 1996.

Chan, Lois Mai, Phyllis A. Richmond, and Elaine Svenonius, eds. *Theory of Subject Analysis: A Sourcebook.* 2d ed. Littleton, Colo.: Libraries Unlimited, 1990.

Clack, Doris Hargrett. *Authority Control: Principles, Applications, and Instructions.* Chicago: American Library Association, 1990.

Commercial Processing Services Committee, Resources and Technical Services Division, American Library Association. "Checklist for Commercial Processing Services." *Library Resources & Technical Services* 23 (Spring 1979): 177–182.

Crawford, Walt. "Introduction to MARC." In *Libraries in the Age of Automation: A Reader for the Professional Librarian.* White Plains, N.Y.: Knowledge Industry Publications, 1986.

———. *MARC for Library Use: Understanding Integrated USMARC.* 2d ed. Boston: G. K. Hall, 1989.

———. *The Online Catalog Book: Essays and Examples.* New York: G. K. Hall, 1992.

Cutter, Charles. *Rules for a Dictionary Catalog.* 4th ed. Washington, D.C.: U.S. Government Printing Office, 1904.

Drabenstott, Karen M., and Marjorie S. Weller. "Handling Spelling Errors in Online Catalog Searches." *Library Resources & Technical Services* 40, no. 2 (April 1996): 113–132.

Edmonds, Leslie, Paula Moore, and Kathleen Mehaffey Balcom. "The Effectiveness of an Online Catalog." *School Library Journal* 36 (October 1990): 28–32.

Ferl, Terry Ellen, and Larry Millsap. *Subject Cataloging: A How-to-Do-It Workbook.* New York: Neal-Schuman, 1991.

Format Integration and Its Effect on the USMARC Bibliographic Format. Washington, D.C.: Library of Congress, Cataloging Distribution Service, 1992.

Foskett, A. C. *The Subject Approach to Information.* 5th ed. London: The Library Association, 1996.

Frost, Carolyn O. *Media Access and Organization: A Cataloging and Reference Sources Guide for Nonbook Materials.* Englewood, Colo.: Libraries Unlimited, 1989.

Furrie, Betty. *Understanding MARC Bibliographic: Machine-Readable Cataloging.* 4th ed. Washington, D.C.: Library of Congress, Cataloging Distribution Service, 1994.

Grosso, Katherine Thompson. "Converting a Catalog from Sears Subject Heading to the Library of Congress Subject Heading." *Illinois Libraries* 62, no. 7 (September 1980): 631–633.

Hagler, Ronald. *The Bibliographic Record and Information Technology.* 3d ed. Chicago: American Library Association, 1997.

Hahn, Harvey. *Technical Services in the Small Library.* Small Libraries Publications, no. 13. Chicago: American Library Association, 1987.

Intner, Sheila S., and Josephine R. Intner. *Technical Services in the Medium-Sized Library.* Hamden, Conn.: Library Professional Publications, 1991.

Librarian's Yellow Pages, '96. Larchmont, N.Y.: Garance, 1996.

Martinez, Michael E. "Access to Information Technologies among School-Age Children: Implications for a Democratic Society." *Journal of the American Society for Information Science* 45, no. 6 (July 1994): 395–400.

Maxwell Robert, and Margaret F. Maxwell. *Maxwell's Handbook for AACR2R, Explaining and Illustrating Anglo-American Cataloguing Rules and the 1993 Amendments.* Chicago: American Library Association, 1997.

Miller, Rosalind E., and Jane C. Terwillegar. *Commonsense Cataloging: A Cataloger's Manual.* 4th ed., rev. New York: H. W. Wilson, 1990.

Moore, Penelope A., and Alison St. George. "Children as Information Seekers: The Cognitive Demands of Books and Library Systems." *School Library Media Quarterly* 19 (Spring 1991): 161–168.

Morrill, Martha. "Roles 2000: How to Contain an Ever-Expanding Job." *School Library Journal* 41, no. 1 (January 1995): 32–34.

"1996 Sourcebook: The Reference for Library Products and Services." Supplement to *Library Journal* (December 1995).

Olson, Nancy B. *Cataloging Computer Files*. Edited by Edward Swanson. Lake Crystal, Mich.: Soldier Creek Press, 1992.

Outsourcing Cataloging, Authority Work, and Physical Processing: A Checklist of Considerations. Chicago: American Library Association, 1995.

Piggott, Mary. *The Cataloguer's Way through AACR2 from Document Receipt to Document Retrieval*. London: The Library Association, 1990.

Rose, Lois Doman. "LC's National Standard for Cataloging Children's Materials." *School Library Journal* 22, no. 5 (January 1976): 20–22.

Sandlian, Pam. "Kid's Catalog: The Global Village Deciphered." *Colorado Libraries* 20 (Spring 1994): 23–25.

Stine, Diane. "Retrospective Conversion Projects." *Media and Methods* (September/October 1996): 33.

Studwell, William E., and David V. Loertscher. *Cataloging Books: A Workbook of Examples*. Englewood, Colo.: Libraries Unlimited, 1989.

Thomsen, Elizabeth B. (March 17, 1995). CL-CAT and Kids: Observations about Children's Searching Skills. Libsplus Discussion Group. [Online] Available e-mail: libsplus@reading.ac.uk

Turner, Treva. "Cataloging Children's Materials at the Library of Congress." *Quarterly Journal of the Library of Congress* 30 (1973): 152–157.

USMARC Format for Bibliographic Data: Including Guidelines for Content Designation. Washington, D.C.: Library of Congress, Cataloging Distribution Service, 1994– .

The USMARC Formats: Background and Principles. Washington, D.C.: Library of Congress, 1989.

Walter, Virginia A., Christine L. Borgman, and Sandra G. Hirsh. "The Science Library Catalog: A Springboard for Information Literacy." *School Library Media Quarterly* 24 (Winter 1996): 105–110.

Weihs, Jean. The *Integrated Library: Encouraging Access to Multimedia Materials*. 2d ed. Phoenix, Ariz.: Oryx Press, 1991.

Weihs, Jean, and Lynne Howarth. *A Brief Guide to AACR2, 1988 Revision, and Implications for Automated Systems*. Ottawa, Ont.: Canadian Library Association, 1988.

Weihs, Jean, with Shirley Lewis. *Nonbook Materials: The Organization of Integrated Collections*. 3d ed. Ottawa, Ont.: Canadian Library Association, 1989; distributed by the American Library Association.

Contributors

Sharon Zuiderveld (Editor) is Staff Librarian and Cataloger at Bound to Stay Bound Books, Inc. in Jacksonville, Illinois. She is former chair of the Cataloging of Children's Materials Committee of ALCTS.

Virginia M. Berringer is Cataloger at the University of Akron Bierce Library in Akron, Ohio.

Ruth Bogan is Authorities Librarian at Cooperative Computer Services in Arlington Heights, Illinois.

Joycelyn Fobes Brand is former Manager and Cataloger of Catalog Card Company in Burnsville, Minnesota. She is a longtime member of the MicroLIF Committee.

John Celli is Chief, Cataloging in Publication, Library of Congress, Washington, D.C.

Frances E. Corcoran is School Library Consultant, currently at the ELA Area Public Library in Lake Zurich, Illinois.

Jane E. Gilchrist is Team Leader of the Children's Literature Team at the History and Cataloging Division of the Library of Congress in Washington, D.C.

Lynne A. Jacobsen is Head of Technical Services at the Warren-Newport Public Library in Gurnee, Illinois.

Joseph Miller is Editor of the *Sears List of Subject Headings* at the H. W. Wilson Company in Bronx, New York.

Catherine Murphy is Assistant Professor at the School of Library and Information Sciences in Denton, Texas.

Gregory R. New is Assistant Editor, Dewey Decimal Classification, Library of Congress, Washington, D.C.

Diane Stine is School Library Consultant at the North Suburban Library System in Wheeling, Illinois.

Pat Thomas is Head Cataloger at the Stockton-San Joaquin County Public Library in Stockton, California.

Betty Vandivier is Cataloging Supervisor of the Instructional Materials Department at the San Diego City Schools in San Diego, California.

Susan Vita is Project Coordinator, Whole Book Cataloging Project, Library of Congress, Washington, D.C. and former Chief, Cataloging in Publication, Library of Congress, Washington, D.C.

Jean Weihs is Principal Consultant at Technical Services Group in Toronto, Ontario, Canada.

Kathleen Wheatley is Youth Services Librarian at the San Diego Public Library in San Diego, California.